INTRODUCTION

Would it surprise you to hear Advent a preparation for it?

Think about it. It would do us no good that Jesus was born as human if we were not reborn as divine. He was born into sharing our lives at Christmas. We were born into sharing his life at Baptism. Baptism is when it all happens for us.

That is why, in every event of Christ's life that we celebrate, we are celebrating the meaning of our Baptism. Learning more about the meaning of our Baptism. Coming to appreciate more the mystery of our Baptism. The mystery of "grace," which is defined as "the favor of sharing in God's own divine life."

The mystery of Baptism is that it is a rebirth through dying and rising in Christ. Unless we understand that, we understand nothing. When we really understand that, we understand everything.

It is really very simple (for a mystery!) if we don't let the time-frame confuse us. Jesus died two thousand years ago. But his death was the central moment of human history. God created the world in view of its redemption through the death and rising of Jesus. Without that, there would have been no point in it. So everything revolves around Jesus. Around his death and resurrection.

Without going into the special power of symbols in liturgy, here's one way to explain it:

For God there is no "before" and "after." There is just one eternal "Now!" So instead of seeing time as a straight line with points on it that are past, present, and future, we can see it as a circle, more like the way God does. God sees everything in time at once, the way we see the whole circle of the moon. On that circle he sees everything that ever happened, is happening, or will happen since the beginning of time.

And the cross of Jesus is at the center of it.

Jesus died in time. But since his death was the moment around which all human history revolves, it is not just an event that took place on the circumference of the circle, about the year 33 A.D. It is also, and above all, a "timeless" moment. The central moment of time. The moment around which time revolves.

And so, in the center of the circle of time we see Jesus, hanging on the cross. And rising. And returning in glory to bring all human history to fulfillment. Jesus is the center of history.

> He is the image of the invisible God, the firstborn of all creation; for in him all things in heaven and on earth were created, things visible and invisible, whether thrones or dominions or rulers or powers—all things have been created through him and for him.
>
> He himself is before all things, and in him all things hold together.

He is the head of the body, the church; he is the beginning, the firstborn from the dead, so that he might come to have first place in everything.

For in him all the fullness of God was pleased to dwell, and through him God was pleased to reconcile to himself all things, whether on earth or in heaven, by making peace through the blood of his cross.[1]

So the death and rising of Jesus is the center of human history. And every event in time is equidistant from it.

That is what a circle is: a line whose two ends meet, and on which every point is the same distance from the center. Jesus is the beginning and end of time, the Alpha and the Omega. And every birth that takes place in time, every point along the circumference of the circle, is equidistant from the center.

When we are baptized, we are baptized *into* the Center, into the body of Jesus hanging on the cross. Baptized into his death. At that moment we die in him and we rise in him. We give up the human lives we received at birth and we receive them back as divine.[2]

We die as humans; we rise as Christ, both human and divine. By Baptism we "become Christ."

Shocking words. But they are the words of St. Augustine, accepted as the official teaching of the Church.[3]

Because we "become Christ," who is the "only Son of the Father," we become sons and daughters of the Father "in Christ." We become true sons and daughters of God. That is why we can pray to God as "*Our Father.*"

And it all happens for us, becomes our reality, at Baptism. That is why, in celebrating the birth of Jesus that made it possible for us to be reborn, we are celebrating our Baptism. That is why, when we celebrate at Mass the death and rising of Jesus that made it possible for us to die and rise in him, we are celebrating our Baptism. That is why, when we pray the "*Our Father,*" we are basing our prayer on our Baptism.

And that is why, as we prepare to celebrate Christmas, we are preparing to celebrate our Baptism.

---

[1] *Colossians* 1:15-20.
[2] *Romans* 6:3-4; *2 Corinthians* 5:14-21.
[3] See *Catechism of the Catholic Church*, no. 795.

First Phrase: *"Our Father…in Heaven"*
First Phase: *Awareness*

Jesus' story about the prodigal son is essentially a story about the father. But it is also a story of the son.[1]

Did the prodigal son really know his father before he left home? Did he really know himself as son?

When the boy asked his father to give him his inheritance, he didn't know his most precious inheritance was simply being the son of his father. He thought it was the property he would receive.

Young fool.

And when he decided to return, he believed that his father would no longer accept him as his son.

> I will go to my father, and say to him, "Father.... I am no longer worthy to be called your son; treat me like one of your hired hands."

He never knew his father until he saw how his father received him back. Until that moment he never knew what it was to be his father's son.

We may be like that young boy.

The "Prodigal Son" is a parable about the mystery of God's "steadfast love." It is also about the Father's inexhaustible forgiveness. But if we look deeper than the act of forgiveness, we find the foundation of *relationship* out of which that forgiveness flowed. We see how God sees himself as our Father. How we should see ourselves as his sons and as his daughters.

It is a principle of philosophy that what we *do* follows from what we *are*. The Father's love follows from the mystery of his *being* as Father and God, and from the mystery of our *being* as "sons and daughters of God." A being we have through baptism.

Most likely that mystery was never sufficiently explained to us. It is the first mystery of baptism, and understanding it is the first step into living our Christian life "to the full."

It is also the first phase of authentic, deep relationship with the God whom we learned to address in the *Gloria* as "almighty God and *Father*"—possibly without addressing what we learned. But when we truly realize who the Father is as our Father, and who we are as his sons and daughters, we will find it a mystical experience to pray, *"Our Father who art in heaven..."*

First Phrase, First Phase:

To experience intimate relationship with the Father, the first thing we need to do is cultivate *awareness* that God has, in fact, become our Father. Our true identity is that we are the sons and daughters of *God*. This identity is not to be taken for granted. It is a mystery—the first mystery of our baptism.

[1] Read *Luke* 15:11-32.

When we call God "Father," this is not some generic identification of all humans as "children of God," or of God as the "father of us all." Even when expressions like these appear in Scripture, outside of the specific revelation made by Jesus, they are words used in metaphor. They mean that, because God is our Creator, the source of our existence, he is "like" a father to us. Or that he treats us as a father would, or deserves from us the reverence we give to our fathers. But as Creator, God is not our father; he is our Creator.[2]

When we say as *Christians*, however, that God is our *Father* and we are his children, we are speaking with the same sense of identity that Jesus himself had. Jesus knew God was his Father in a unique way, beyond anything anyone had ever claimed or dreamed of before. Whether or not he could have spelled it out explicitly in his human consciousness, the truth is, Jesus *was* God. He was "God the Son" by nature, second Person of the Blessed Trinity, the unique, the *only* Son of the Father. He declared explicitly and emphatically that his relationship to the Father was unique: "*No one* knows the Son except the Father, and no one knows the Father except the Son." To know the Son as "Son," you would have to *be* the Father. To know the Father as "Father," you would have to *be* the Son. Quite simply, to know God as God you have to be God.[3]

That is why, when Jesus continued, in apparent self-contradiction, "No one knows the Father except the Son *and anyone to whom the Son chooses to reveal him*," he was announcing that those who received the "grace of the Lord Jesus Christ" would become God! They would become the Son by sharing in his own life—in his own unique, divine life and knowledge. They would know the Father as their Father in the only way possible: by sharing in the Son's own act of knowing the Father as his own. They would know him as *filii in Filio*, sons and daughters *in the Son*. They would "become God" by "becoming Christ."

Shocking words, but accepted phrases in Church writings. Every year we read the words of Blessed Isaac of Stella in the *Liturgy of the Hours*: "Those who by faith are spiritual members of Christ can truly say that they *are what he is*: the Son of God *and God himself!*"

Father Michael Casey, a Trappist monk of Tarrawarra in Australia, wrote: "Ac-

---

[2]See, for example, *1 Chronicles* 17:13-14; *Acts* 17:28-29. Ray Brown wrote that the *"Our Father"* is "a Christian prayer; for despite the vague modern use of the 'fatherhood of God,' it is the New Testament outlook that only those have God as a Father who recognize Jesus as his Son." *New Testament Essays*, "The *Pater Noster* as an Eschatological Prayer," Doubleday/Image, 1968, p. 283.

An "expansion of remarks" for those who want to go deeper: The artist who paints a picture is not the "father" of that image. The artist is intellectual flesh and blood; the image is inanimate canvas and paint. The difference between what God is and what we are, even created in his image, is infinitely greater than that.

God is God, Being Itself, who has within himself the source of his own existence. We are creatures, brought to be out of nothingness, whose existence here and now depends on God's ongoing, continuing act of creation. When God says, "Be," what his word brings into existence continues to exist only so long as God "holds the note." Provided we understand that our created existence is distinct from his, we can say that our existence is simply an ongoing action of God. We *are* only as long as he is creating us. Our being is God saying, "Beeeee...." That makes God our Creator, not our father.

[3]See *Matthew* 11:25-27.

cording to the teaching of many Church Fathers, particularly those of the East, *Christian life consists not so much in being good as in becoming God."*

He continues, commenting on the beginning of John's Gospel: "Everything the Word was by nature, we become by grace."[4]

St. Augustine, quoted in the *Catechism of the Catholic Church* (no. 795), insists, speaking to the baptized: "We are not just Christians; we have *become Christ.*" And he repeats it: "Wonder and marvel: we have *become Christ.*"

We have not truly heard the Good News, we have not been fully "evangelized," until we are able to say with awe and wonder, "The Father of Jesus Christ is *my Father.* I have *become Christ.* In him, I am a son or daughter *in the Son of God.*"

"Son of Man, Son of God"

Jesus commonly (78 times) referred to himself in the Gospels as the "Son of Man." This was an indirect way of calling himself the Son of God. It implied Jesus was not just a "son of man" as we are. For a native-born citizen of the United States to take as a title "the American" would not make sense; it would be to enunciate the obvious. But if a naturalized citizen took that title, it would tell us that originally he or she was something else. The title "Son of Man" tells us that Jesus *became* the Son of Man. But from the beginning, by nature he was something else. He was the Son of God, meaning "God the Son, Second Person of the Blessed Trinity." He was truly Son of Man, but secondarily, by taking on human nature. "In the beginning was the Word, and the Word was with God, and the Word was God." But then "the Word was made flesh" and became the "Son of Man."[5]

For a Christian to say, "I am the Son of God," is to use the title as Jesus used "Son of Man." We are truly *filii in Filio*, "sons and daughters in the Son," but in a secondary sense. We were not this "from the beginning." We *became* children of the Father, as the Word "became flesh." We could not assume the nature of God in the same way the Word assumed human nature (no creature could), but by Baptism we became true *sharers* in the divine nature and life of God, and therefore true "sons and daughters of the Father." Having become this, we cannot understand ourselves or our relationship to God or to the world in any other way. If asked who we are, our most accurate response would be to say, "I am the son (or daughter) of God."

To say, "I am a Christian" does not just mean I believe in Christ or follow him. It means I have been "christified." I have *become Christ.* To say "I am a Chris-

[4]See his book, *Fully Human, Fully Divine*, "Preface," pp. vii and 9-10 (Liguori/Triumph, 2004). Blessed Isaac of Stella is quoted in the *Liturgy of the Hours*, second reading, Friday, fifth week of Easter. With Bl. Isaac, Fr. Michael adds some theological precisions: "Each of the believing and reasoning members of Christ can truly say of themselves that they are what he is—even God's Son, even God. But he is so by nature, they by [partnership or] association (*consortio*). He is so fully; they by participation. Finally, what the Son is by virtue of being begotten his members are... by adoption." That is why we specify in the Profession of Faith that Jesus is the "only *begotten* Son of the Father." But this "adoption" is itself a mystery. God makes us his children, not just by a legal decree or by the giving of a name, but by a true bestowal of his own life on us.
[5]This is not a scholarly exegesis of "Son of Man," whose meaning in the Gospel usage is disputed and complex. See J. McKenzie, S.J., *Dictionary of the Bible.*

tian" is to announce a mystery. The mystery is "the grace of the Lord Jesus Christ," which means the *favor* of *sharing in the divine life of God.*

If we had a true understanding of our identity, we would think of ourselves, speak of ourselves, and logically introduce ourselves (when socially feasible) as "the son/daughter of God." This should constitute our basic self-awareness. It is the mystery of our being. Unless we understand that we have "become Christ," we do not understand that we are Christians.

And we cannot pray, *"Our Father who art in heaven"* as Jesus meant us to pray.

That is why it is so important to *remain aware* of who God is and who we are. This is the first thing to cultivate in our journey to the Father.

Tools of the Trade

When we acknowledge and accept God as our Father, we are keenly aware that we are called to live and act as his Son. As Jesus. Because we have "become Christ," we need to live on the level of God. St. John wrote, "Whoever says, 'I abide in him,' ought to walk just as he walked." For this we turn to the Spirit.[6]

The *Our Father* involves us with the Three Persons of the Blessed Trinity. When we pray to the Father, taking on the priorities of Jesus as our goals in its petitions, we naturally turn to God the Son, who alone can bring about these goals, and who was sent to do it. We offer him our bodies, as we did at Baptism, and ask him: "Live this day *with* me, live this day *in* me, live this day *through* me."

But for Jesus to do this, we have to cooperate. And we know we can't cooperate with him as we should without empowerment by the Holy Spirit. So we turn to the Spirit, who is called in the Mass God's "first gift" to those who believe, the "first fruits" of redemption. *"Come, Holy Spirit, fill the hearts of the faithful...."*

The Spirit responds by empowering us through the "Gifts of the Holy Spirit." The first and most fundamental of these is *"Fear of the Lord."*[7]

"Fear of the Lord" is the gift of awe and reverence for what God is, combined with deep recognition of what we are—and are not.

Imagine fear without the emotion of fright. What is left is *perspective*. An electrician working on high-tension wires is not "afraid." But no one should do that job without a keen sense of perspective: a strong awareness of how much power is in those wires, and what it is able to do to something as fragile as a human body. No one who has this sense of perspective is going to take any risks.

An old cowboy in Texas said about horses: "You can't be scared of 'em, but you gotta treat 'em with respect." To take this attitude toward God is "fear of the Lord." When this fear is the divine Gift of Fear, our perspective is clarified by divine enlightenment: we see the infinite Being of God as only God himself can see it. We see him as our All: as all Goodness, all Truth, all Power. Without terror, we see that to go against God is insanity. There is no good to hope for apart from him, no fulfillment of any sort except in union with him. This is the

---

[6]See *1 John* 2:6.
[7]See *Eucharistic Prayer IV*. The "Gifts of the Spirit" are: Wisdom, Understanding, Knowledge, Counsel, Piety, Fortitude, and Fear of the Lord. See *Isaiah* 11:1-3; *Catechism of the Catholic Church*, nos. 1930-1831.

Fear of the Lord that makes us accept the First Commandment as obvious: "You shall love the Lord your God with *all* your heart, and with *all* your soul, and with *all* your mind." This becomes for us our personal "greatest and first commandment," the basic, all-determining rule we live by.⁸

As the gift of perspective, *Fear of the Lord* also makes us aware that of ourselves we are nothing. Literally. If I look at the hand in front of my face, I see no reason why it should exist. It does exist, but it does not have within itself anything that explains that fact. When God gives existence to a creature, he cannot make that existence self-explanatory or self-sustaining, independent of his continuing act of creation. It just isn't. For my hand—for my person—to make sense as existing, there must be some Source, some Cause of my existence whose Existence does not need any explanation, because its very Nature is to Be. A Being that has within itself the explanation of its own Existence. A Being who is All.

This is the way God identified himself when Moses asked his Name. God answered, "I Am Who Am." I am the one who just Is, because it is impossible, inconceivable, for me not to Be.⁹

God said to St. Catherine of Siena, "I am He who Is; you are she who is not." To recognize this is the "other end" of *Fear of the Lord*. To see God in perspective as All, we must see ourselves in perspective as essentially nothing.

THE ENEMY

Fear of the Lord is truth. To accept truth is humility. Humility is defined as "being peaceful with the truth." It is the antidote for *Pride*. Pride is the worst of all the "Capital Sins" because it is the ultimate falsification. It makes us like the devil, the "father of lies."

The truly "proud" don't just see themselves as "better" than they are; that can be simply "vanity," which is mostly misinformation. Pride is to *make ourselves the criterion*. It is only vanity to judge we are smarter than we actually are. But vanity becomes pride when we assume we are so smart that *whatever we think must be true*. Or believe we are so good that whatever we are inclined to do must be right. That is to make ourselves the criterion. It is to make ourselves "like God"—not through the free gift of sharing in his divine life, which is grace, but through the blind presumption of declaring ourselves to be what we are not.¹⁰

THE BEGINNING OF WISDOM

In Scripture *Fear of the Lord* is called "the beginning of *Wisdom*."¹¹

St. Thomas Aquinas defines *Wisdom* in two ways: as the "Gift of the Spirit" that lets us *appreciate* spiritual things; and as the *habit* of seeing everything in the

---

⁸Clarity about who God is as the All involves the Gift of Understanding, just as making the First Commandment our personal rule of life involves the Gift of Wisdom, by which we see everything in the light of our last end. Assigning particular gifts to particular phases of our spiritual growth is emphasis rather than exclusivity.
⁹*Exodus* 3:13-14.
¹⁰See *Matthew* 5:3. See also the theme of *bajeza*, lowliness, in St. Ignatius of Loyola; e.g. the "Three Kinds of Humility," *Spiritual Exercises*, nos. 165-168; and the *Rule of St. Benedict*, chapter; 7.
¹¹*Proverbs* 9:10.

light of our last end. They are the same reality: if our divine understanding of God as All Good (*Fear of the Lord*) moves us to direct everything in our lives toward union and possession of him, we will have a keen appreciation for everything "spiritual" that helps us do that. So *Fear of the Lord* is the beginning of *Wisdom*. It is the beginning, the foundation of our whole spiritual life. It is the first "tool of the trade" we receive that helps us live authentically as Christians.

FEAR AND SIN

Fear of the Lord is our first protection against sin. This is not primarily because we are "afraid of his just punishments." That kind of fear is an authentic, but low-level, experience of fear of the Lord. We should not despise or underestimate its value.[12] But if, with mature fear of the Lord we see God in *perspective* as the source and reality of all good, then to choose any apparent good that separates or even distances us from him is by definition self-destructive. Stupidity. Diminishment. Suicide. If the prodigal son had made himself aware of how good he had it with his father, he would never have left him. That is authentic *Fear of the Lord*.

The liturgy reminds us of this: "Every good thing comes from you.... Nothing is good which is against your will; and all is of value which comes from your hand." And "There is no power for good that does not come from your covenant, and no promise to hope in that your love has not offered."[13]

Seen in this perspective, nothing can tempt us. If anything does, we have lost perspective. So the first requirement for living the Christian life is to cultivate and maintain *awareness*. The more that, by the gift of *Fear of the Lord*, we remain aware of who God is and who we are—the less anything can allure us away from God or tempt us to go against his will.

This explains why sin is impossible in heaven, even though we remain free. When we see God face-to-face, not only recognizing, but experiencing and possessing him as All Good, nothing outside of him can even appear to have anything to offer us. Nothing can attract those who are already in total possession of the All.

That is why it is so important to *remain aware* of who God is and who we are. This is the first thing to cultivate in our journey to the Father.

THE SON'S RETURN

Let's fantasize. The prodigal son is returning home. But instead of his father, a servant meets him at the gate. The servant says, "Come in; your father is waiting for you." Then he takes him to a part of the farm the son has never seen before, because it was off limits to everyone, hidden behind a thick growth of trees where there were always a pair of "gardeners" who made sure no one passed through.

The servant takes him through the trees, and before his eyes he sees a palace. More splendid than anything he could ever imagine.

"What is that?" he asks the servant.

---

[12] See St. Ignatius of Loyola's meditation on Hell, *Spiritual Exercises*, no. 61.
[13] Opening Prayers for the Twenty-Second and Thirtieth Sundays of Ordinary Time.

"That is your father's palace. You thought he was just a farmer. That is what he wanted you to think, so you would grow up without any pretensions. But the truth is, he is the king of all this country, and this is the place he would disappear to when you thought he was making trips. This is where he reigns as king."

The boy is flabbergasted. As they enter the palace, they walk through one room after another of unimaginable splendor. He is open-mouthed with awe and wonder. Then they arrive at the throne room.

It is an immense hall, all in marble inset with gold and jewels. Tapestries of incalculable value hang from the ceiling. Around the walls a thousand guards are standing, their liveries so rich they dazzle the eyes. And in the center of the room is his father.

His father is seated on a throne of gold from which reflected light is shining so brilliantly he appears to be surrounded by a bright cloud. All around him the lords and ladies of the realm are kneeling, doing him homage. Voices are lifted up in praise: "Glory and honor to the King! To our ruler seated on the throne be blessing and honor and glory and might forever and ever!"

The boy is awestruck. He becomes painfully conscious of his clothes, still spattered with the filth of the pig sty. He realizes he has never known his father, never seen him in a true perspective, never dreamed he was so far above himself and everyone around him. He begins to back out of the room. Isn't that what anyone would do?

Dignitaries generate distance. Splendor separates. Majesty is foreign to familiarity. The more exalted we see another to be, the more lowly we appear in our own eyes.

But then that is reversed. The king steps down from his throne, calls his son to himself, kisses him, embraces him, makes him sit beside him on his throne.

Everything changes. The bright cloud of splendor that overawed and excluded now appears as an including, enfolding embrace of familiarity and welcome. That which was exclusive and unique to a king now becomes the lap of a father and the boy's natural environment. All that was different and kept the son at a distance is now an inherited characteristic of the son himself. He shares his father's glory.

When our "return to our Father" is complete, we will realize that anything negative in our *"Fear of the Lord"* came from an incomplete perception of our Father. All that kept us at a distance from God we will now enter into as our own inheritance. We who feared to approach God the Almighty, God the All powerful, God the Lord of heaven and earth, will now run to him like children snuggling into the lap of their Father.

This is what it means to say, *"Our Father... in heaven."*

Awareness: Heaven Inside of Us

Teresa of Avila writes of how important it is, not only to believe in this mystery of God's life, God's presence in us, but also to remain *aware* of it. She calls this "recollection," and defines it as the soul "collecting together all its faculties and entering within itself to be with its God." She explains that we need to "truly understand that we have within ourselves something incomparably more precious than anything we see outside ourselves."

To be conscious of God within us, however, we have to stop "pouring ourselves out" on everything outside of us. (The spiritual writers call this *effusio ad exteriorem*). We need to stop being dependent on constant input from ipods and cell phones, car radios and TV, whose effect is to draw us out of self-awareness. We need to listen, even in the midst of our ordinary occupations, to the "sounds of silence" coming from our souls.

> You will laugh at me, perhaps, and say that what I am explaining is very clear.... For me, though, it was obscure for some time. I understood that I had a soul. But what this soul deserved, and who dwelt within it I did not understand until I closed my eyes to the vanities of this world in order to see it. I think, if I had understood then, as I do now, how this great King *really* dwells within this little palace of my soul, I should not have left him alone so often, but should have stayed with him....
>
> All the harm comes from not really grasping the fact that he is near to us, and imagining him far away—so far that we shall have to go to heaven in order to find him....
>
> The truth is, "We have heaven within ourselves since the Lord of Heaven is there."[14]

ONE SIMPLE SUGGESTION

The first phase in the process of "making our own" the mystery of Baptism, is to cultivate *awareness*—constant awareness of who we are. And this means to be conscious of who is *with* us. Who is *in* us. Who wants to be acting *through* us in everything we do. Awareness of *being Christ*, of being sons and daughters of the Father "in the Son," of being *divine*, of being called, committed, and empowered to *live on the level of God*, is the first level, the first stage, the first phase of our growth into the fullness of Christian life. It is our "first step to the Father."

How do we do it? There is a very simple way. It is not difficult and it costs nothing. It doesn't even take up time. It is to say the WIT prayer. W. I. T.

When you wake up in the morning, before you even open your eyes, say, "Lord, I give you my body. Live this day *with* me; live this day *in* me; live this day *through* me."

"*With me*": You are never alone. Jesus is always "at your side." This inspired the Christian refrain, "The Lord be with you."

"*In me*": More than that, he is *within* you. We are going deeper into mystery. Jesus dwells in you, "abides" in you, together with the Father and the Spirit. This is the mystery of our being:

> Father, may they be one, as we are one, *I in them and you in me*.... I will ask the Father, and he will give you another Advocate, to be with you forever....The Spirit of truth... You know him, *because he abides with you*, and he will be *in you*...
>
> Those who love me will keep my word, and my Father will love them, and we will come to them and *make our home with them*.... Abide in me as I abide in you.

[14]*The Way of Perfection*, chapters 28, 29. What I haven't translated from the Spanish is from E. Allison Peers, Image Books edition, 1964; and *The Collected Works*, vol. 2, tr. Kieran Kavanaugh, O.C.D. and Otilio Rodriguez, O.C.D., ICS Publications, Institute of Carmelite Studies, 1980.

Those who eat my flesh and drink my blood *abide in me, and I in them*.[15]

This was a theme song for St. John:

> Let what you heard from the beginning abide in you. [Be *aware* of it]. If what you heard from the beginning abides in you, then *you will abide in the Son and in the Father*.
>
> And now, little children, *abide in him*. *God abides* in those who confess that Jesus is the Son of God, and *they abide in God*.
>
> All who obey his commandments *abide in him, and he abides in them*.... By this we know that *we abide in him and he in us*, because he has given us of his Spirit.
>
> So we have known and believe the love that God has for us. God is love, and *those who abide in love abide in God, and God abides in them*.[16]

"Through me." Jesus is not with us and in us just to help us do "our thing." He wants to do "his thing," his divine thing, by acting through us, through our physical words and actions. We are his body. We exist to let him act with us, in us, and through us to continue his mission in the world.

WIT: *With, in, through*. Saying the WIT prayer, and saying it all day long, before everything we do, keeps us conscious of his presence in us. His presence uniting us to himself, giving us a new identity, making all that we do "in him" divine.

We just need to form the habit of saying this prayer all day long.

To form the habit, in the beginning we may have to use reminders. A handkerchief on the doorknob. Or on the telephone. A cross attached to our car keys. A medal or crucifix in our pocket or purse. A glass of water on our desk that to us alone speaks of Baptism. An Easter palm in the utensils drawer, or blocking access to what is in the kitchen cupboard. A Bible next to the coffeepot (at home), or a less explicit symbol at work. A coffee cup with a logo. The word WIT in our password or on our screensaver. A card on top of the keyboard. Be creative. Saturate your senses.

Other reminders come naturally. Whenever we feel nervous about something we need to do, we counter the anxiety by saying: "Lord, do this with me; do this in me; do this through me." When we feel we are going to speak with impatience or anger, we pray: "Lord, say this with me; say this in me; say this through me."

To do *consciously* what is divine is a mystical experience. It is conscious awareness of living out the mystery of our Baptism. Awareness makes the mystery real. The mystery of being truly (and truly being) the Son of God. The Daughter of God. Of being divine. Of "being God" because we have "become Christ."

This is the first mystery of Baptism. It is all contained in the words, *"Our Father…in heaven."* To absorb it, just form the habit of saying the WIT prayer all day long. It will transform your life.[17]

---

[15] See *John* 6:56; 14:16-17, 23; 15:4; 17:22-23.
[16] See *1 John* 2:24-28; 3:24; 4:13-16.
[17] Don't take my word for it. Read the spiritual classic: *The Practice of the Presence of God*, by the Carmelite Brother Lawrence of the Resurrection (born in France, 1614; died 1691). Critical edition by Conrad de Meester, OCD, ICS Publications, Institute of Carmelite Studies, Washington, D.C., 1994.

SUNDAY   First Sunday of Advent

NOVEMBER 27, 2011
The Beginning of Religion

Lord, make us turn to you.
Let us see your face and we shall be saved.
(Responsorial: Psalm 80)

INVENTORY

What is the very first act of religion? When and where did it take place in your life? How did you experience it? How often are you conscious of it now?

The *Entrance Antiphon* tells us the first and basic act of religion is: *"To you, my God, I lift up my soul."* The *Responsorial Psalm* echoes it: *turning to God*, seeking contact with him, is the beginning of that conscious relationship with God we call "religion." This is our focus as we enter into Advent.

INPUT

The *Opening Prayer* presupposes the Good News that God has "turned to us" to initiate the religious relationship we call "Christianity." He has done more than turn to us; he has *come* to us in Jesus, God made flesh. And so we pray that Jesus will "find an eager welcome" in our hearts when we celebrate that coming at Christmas.

The prayer includes a reference to Christ's Second Coming at the end of the world. We ask that he will "call us to his side in the kingdom of heaven, where he lives and reigns" with the Father and Spirit. Advent is rich with a double meaning; it focuses on the beginning and the end: the inauguration of Christianity at Christ's birth; the fulfillment of Christianity at the end of the world when he returns in triumph. The same two comings bracket the Mass, which begins with the angels' Christmas song in the *Gloria*: "Glory to God in the highest heaven, and on earth peace among those whom he favors!" and ends with the "second advent" prayer during the *Rite of Communion*: that God will "deliver us from every evil... as we await the blessed hope and the coming (*adventum*) of our Savior, Jesus Christ."[1]

The *Responsorial Psalm* echoes this prayer as it gives the theme of the readings: *Lord, make us turn to you. Let us see your face and we shall be saved.* The readings from *Isaiah* and *1 Corinthians* tell us what we expect to see when he comes: what being "saved" means. The reading from Mark's Gospel warns us that we don't know *when* he will return, so if we want to be saved we should be awake and watching. Advent is an invitation to come to terms with all of that.

---

[1] See *Luke* 2:14; *Titus* 2:13. St. Jerome's Latin Vulgate translates the Greek *epiphanaian* ("manifestation") as *adventum*, which means "arrival" or "coming."

First Sunday of Advent — SUNDAY

Our "Father"

Isaiah 63:16 to 64:7 begins with what "salvation" is all about: "You, O LORD, are our father. Redeemer is your name."

When Isaiah used the term "father," for him it only meant "Creator":

> O Lord, you are our father; we are the clay, and you are the potter; we are all the work of your hands.

This is a metaphorical use of "father." But for Christians the meaning is literal. Jesus came to make God our real Father: the one who is not only the cause of our existence, but whose life determines what our life is. The life we have by grace is divine, because it is the Life of God himself. This is a mystery, and it is essential that we understand it. Otherwise, we have not really "heard" the Good News.

The "grace" that Jesus came to give us is the *favor* of *sharing in the divine life of God*. Not in a life *like* God's. Not in some created imitation or replica of God's divine life. God's life cannot be duplicated. It is unique. Infinite. Indivisible. The only way anyone can have *divine* life is by sharing in the life God is actually living, as he lives it. By union with him. What kind of union?

This is union on the level of *being*, not just of operation. Creatures can only be united by *acting* on or with each other; for example, sharing in each other's thoughts through communication, singing a song in harmony, carrying a box together. Only God can unite us to himself on the level of *being*.

And when he does, since this union is on a level prior to operation; that is, since we are one with God *before* we begin to *act*, all that we do in "grace" is both human and divine. When we love someone by grace, there is only one act of love. But it is both God's act of love and ours combined in one single divine-human act of loving.

When we love in grace, Jesus Christ loves *with us, in us, and through us*. And we love *through him, with him, and in him*. And since the Father, Son, and Spirit all act together, united in the divine Life they share, the Father and Spirit are loving in us also.

This is the mystery of the "grace of the Lord Jesus Christ" that we announce at the beginning of every Mass to remind us of who and what we are. This, brought to fullness, is the "salvation" we will see shining in the face of Jesus when he comes. This is what Advent reminds us to look forward to as we "await the blessed hope and the coming of our Savior, Jesus Christ." We need to ponder this mystery until it excites us!

"Fellowship" with Christ

1 Corinthians 1:3-9 summons us to come to terms with this "favor" that God has "bestowed on us in Christ Jesus." What does it mean that God has called us into "fellowship" with his Son Jesus? This is the basic reality of our Christian life. We need to understand it.

The word "fellowship" (*koinonia*) is better translated "communion." It is not the fellowship of "hail fellows well met" that we experience at parties and class reunions. Christian *koinonia* is a "common union," a common "participation in Christ, in the Spirit, in the divine nature, in the same life of faith." It is a mystery; the mystery of sharing—with Christ and with each other—in the divine life of God.[1]

Jesus is not just our Lord, Teacher, Leader, or "Messiah" as the word was

SUNDAY   First Sunday of Advent

understood before he came. Paul says that even we, who "have been richly endowed with every gift of speech and knowledge" are still "waiting for the revelation of our Lord Jesus Christ." We know and we don't know who he is. We have seen and not seen his glory.[2]

Jesus is not just God made human. He is more of a mystery than the manger scene at Christmas can begin to express.

> He is... the firstborn of all creation; for in him all things in heaven and on earth were created... In him all things hold together.
>
> He is the head of the body, the church; he is the beginning, the firstborn from the dead.... Through him God was pleased to reconcile to himself all things....

He is the head of the body of which we are members. He is the vine, we are the branches. We are true sons and daughters of the Father, of his Father, because we are "in him." This is "the mystery that has been hidden throughout the ages and generations but has now been revealed": that *we are in Christ and Christ is in us*. This is our "hope of glory."

We don't even know who we are, really, and won't until "Christ who is our life is revealed. Then we also will be revealed with him in glory."[3]

Does this give us a reason to do some thinking during Advent? "Turn our face" to him? Read something? Participate in a discussion group? Take time for reflective prayer? *Lord, make us turn to you. Let us see your face and we shall be saved.*

WAKE-UP!

Mark 13:33-37 calls us to wake up! To be aware. Jesus doesn't just come at Christmas and at the end of the world. He comes to each one of us every day, many times a day. And he comes for the same reason he came at Christmas: to save us. To save us from veering off to a mediocre family and social life, or to meaningless business and professional activity. He comes in the form of thoughts, inspirations, challenges—all inviting us to live "life to the full."

Jesus said that this is what he came for: that we might "have life and have it to the full." And he specified: "This is eternal life, that they may *know you, the only true God*, and Jesus Christ whom you have sent." Is getting to know God better my main preoccupation in life?[4]

If it isn't, I have work to do in Advent: *Lord, make us turn to you. Let us see your face and we shall be saved.* In my own life, what would it mean, in the concrete, to "turn to him"?

---

[1]See Xavier Leon-Dufour, S.J., *Dictionary of the New Testament*, Harper & Row, 1983.
[2]Cp. *John* 1:14; 17:5, 24; *Matthew* 16:27; 24:30.
[3]*Matthew* 12:47-50; *Romans* 12:4-5; *1 Corinthians* 12:12-27; *Colossians* 1:15-28; 3:4; *John* 15:5; 20:17.
[4]*John* 10:10; 17:3.

INSIGHT
What am I looking forward to during Advent? Do I think I really understand the mystery of Christ? Am I letting him "save" my home life? Professional life?

INITIATIVE:
Ask seriously: "How can I use the time of Advent to become a happier person?"

First Week of Advent Monday

November 28, 2011

Let us go rejoicing to the house of the Lord.
(Responsorial: Psalm 122)

The *Responsorial* is the key to the readings. If we have heard the Good News that God has "made us turn to him" that we might "see his face and be saved" (see Sunday) the obvious response is: *Let us go rejoicing to the house of the Lord.* If we do not go rejoicing, we have not heard the Good News. Then Advent should have special urgency for us.

Isaiah 2:1-5 tells us why we should *go rejoicing to the house of the Lord.* It is because "the mountain of the Lord's house shall be established as the highest of the mountains, and... all the nations shall stream to it." For what?

> That he may teach us his ways and that we may walk in his paths. For out of Zion shall go forth instruction, and the word of the LORD from Jerusalem.

We *go rejoicing to the house of the Lord* so that we might *know God.* It is to "see his face and be saved." The two go together. Jesus said, "This is eternal life, that they may *know you*...."[1]

"Eternal life" is not the same as "everlasting life." Only God has Life that is eternal: without beginning and without end. And this Life is ours by "the grace of the Lord Jesus Christ." Because we are "in Christ" by Baptism, we share in the divine life of God.

This is the only way we can truly "know the Father." Jesus was explicit about this: "No one knows—or could possibly know—the Father except the Son." To know God as God, the Father as Father, the Son as Son, is what it means to *be God.* When Jesus added, "and anyone to whom the Son chooses to reveal him." He was defining the "grace of the Lord Jesus Christ" as the favor of sharing in God's own divine life. Eternal life. "This is eternal life, that they may *know you*, the only true God." So *let us go rejoicing to the house of the Lord*, that he may teach us his ways.[2]

In **Matthew 8:5-11** directions are reversed. Jesus is "going to the house" of a Roman centurion. When the centurion declares his faith that Jesus can cure his servant by just speaking a word, Jesus reverses the direction again. He declares to us that the centurion has just entered into the "house of the Lord." When the centurion "saw his face" with faith, he was saved:

> Truly I tell you... many will come from east and west and will find a place at the banquet in the kingdom of God with Abraham, Isaac and Jacob...

The Gospel text continues:

> And to the centurion Jesus said, "Go; let it be done for you according to your faith." And the servant was healed in that hour.

Advent invites us to have faith. And to increase the faith we do have by "seeing the face" of Jesus more clearly. For this we have to *look* at him. And let's be honest: How often do we do that?

Advent is a time to *go to the house of the Lord* and invite him into our house.

[1] *John* 10:10; 17:3.
[2] *Matthew* 11:27.

Initiative: Be aware of the face of God as revealed. Read Scripture. Daily.

Tuesday First Week of Advent

November 29, 2011

Justice shall flourish in our time, and fullness of peace forever.
(Responsorial: Psalm 72)

"Knowing the Father" sounds like a pretty mystical experience. And it is one. It is the experience of sharing in God's own act of knowing himself. That is the definition of "faith."

We can be aware of this knowledge. Experience is by definition awareness. But the awareness may be indirect. That is, we are aware of knowing God, not because we see him clearly in some vivid intellectual vision, but because we are aware that there is something in our life that cannot be explained if we don't know him. Ultimately, what cannot be humanly explained is the deep, absolute *certitude* we have that there is a God and that he is our Father.

That certitude is not the same as a felt conviction. In the "dark night of the soul," the spiritual masters tell us, God is "just a three-letter word." We feel that we have no faith at all. What gives the lie to that feeling is the way we are living. If it doesn't make sense without God, we know we believe.

Anyone who knows God as Father will have the spirit **Isaiah 11:1-10** attributes to the Son:

> The spirit of the LORD shall rest on him, the spirit of wisdom and understanding, the spirit of counsel and might, the spirit of knowledge and the fear of the LORD.

The result of them all is "peace":

> They will not hurt or destroy on all my holy mountain; for the earth will be full of the knowledge of the LORD as the waters cover the sea.

Jesus said, "Blessed are the peacemakers, for they will be called children of God." When we treat all, friends and enemies alike, as our brothers and sisters, we will know we know God as our Father. *Justice shall flourish in our time, and fullness of peace forever.*

In **Luke 10:21-24** Jesus wants to give us reassurance. We don't have to be "learned and clever" to know the Father. God has revealed himself to the "merest children."

> Yes, Father, you have graciously willed it so.

In Matthew's version, these words are followed by:

> Come to me, all you that are weary and are carrying heavy burdens, and I will give you rest. Take my yoke upon you, and learn from me; for I am gentle and humble in heart, and you will find rest for your souls. For my yoke is easy, and my burden is light.

Any teacher in the Church who makes God or our religion look harsh simply does not know the Father. Jesus condemned those of his time who focused on law-observance:

> Woe to you Pharisees.... Woe also to you lawyers! For you load people with burdens hard to bear, and you yourselves do not lift a finger to ease them.

If we find religion burdensome, or do not find comfort in thinking of our Father, we should rethink what we have learned. When we understand, *"Justice shall flourish in our time, and fullness of peace forever."*

Initiative: Be aware of your experience of the Father. Go deep in your heart.

Feast of Saint Andrew, Apostle — Wednesday

November 30, 2011

Their message goes out through all the earth.
(*Responsorial: Psalm* 19)

In **Romans 10:9-18** Paul is painstakingly precise about process. "Salvation" begins with "the *word* of Christ" (cp. John's Gospel; "In the beginning was the Word"). Then someone has to be *sent*. This implies *preaching*; which people have to *hear*. If those who hear *believe* they can *ask his help*, "everyone who calls on the name of the Lord will be saved." But there is one more requirement. "By believing from the heart you are made righteous," but it is only "by *confessing with your lips* [that] you are saved."

That adds up to seven steps: the *word* given, someone *sent*, *preaching*, *hearing*, *believing*, *asking* God's help, and *confessing with the lips*. Take a moment to identify when and how each one of these became present in your life.

Do you consciously ground your faith in the *word* of God? Or was that awareness just buried somewhere as background in the religious instruction you received? Or buried in an unreflective acceptance of the Catholic culture you grew up in?

Were you aware that those who taught you were *sent* by God? Did you listen to them with the awe and respect owed to messengers from God? Were you aware *God* was talking to you through them?

How did you listen to the *preaching* you heard? As a child, a teenager, were you listening as a "disciple," someone intent on learning, or just as an "audience" waiting for something to "hit" you? How do you listen today?

Above all, were you consciously aware of *believing* what you heard, of responding to it with a personal, conscious act of faith? Were you aware of listening with a mind empowered to believe with the *gift* of divine enlightenment that we call "faith"—a gift included, with hope and love, in the gift of divine life that we call "grace"?

Do you appreciate how far beyond human powers it is to believe and follow the word of God? Do you *ask God's help*, saying, "Lord, I believe; help my unbelief"? Or do you just take your ability to be a Christian for granted?[1]

Finally, did you appreciate how important it is to *confess with your lips* that you believe, trust in God, love God as your all and Jesus as your Way, your Truth, your Life?[2]

How often now do you explicitly "confess with your lips" your relationship to God? Do you sing at Mass? Consciously join in the responses? Do you recite or sing the *Gloria* like a "pledge of allegiance," proclaiming your faith and your commitment? Do you follow and echo in your heart all the words the presider at Mass says aloud in your name?

Matthew 4:18-22. You heard the Good News because others answered this call. Have you answered it too?

[1] *Mark* 9:24.
[2] *John* 14:6.

Initiative: Take seriously the gift of faith. Profess it and share it.

THURSDAY FIRST WEEK OF ADVENT

DECEMBER 1, 2011

Blessed is he who comes in the name of the Lord!
(Responsorial: *Psalm* 118)

Advent is a looking forward to the coming of Jesus: at Christmas, at the end of the world, and at death, which is the practical "end" for each of us. The question is, do we look forward to it? Do we, can we, sincerely say: *Blessed is he who comes in the name of the Lord!*

All religion is meant to encourage, to give us confidence. When it doesn't, then either something is wrong with us or wrong with the way we understand our religion. Or both.

Isaiah 26:1-6 speaks of the security we find with God: "A strong city have we.... Trust in the Lord forever!" He affirms this, however, as the blessing of those who are in *relationship* with God:

> A nation that is just, one that keeps faith... you keep in peace, for its trust is in you.

This relationship does not presuppose that we are strong people, in such control of ourselves that we never fall into sin. That is desirable, of course, but also dangerous. It can lead us into the self-righteous pride of the Pharisees.

Committing sin is not the antidote! It is to avoid "high places"—honors, position, prestige (even in our own minds) that make us think we have the "higher ground" compared to others. No matter how successful we are—even in keeping God's law—we need to see ourselves always as identified with the "needy" and "poor."

We need not fear to do this. Any confidence we place in ourselves, including our good behavior, is skating on thin ice. We have only one true and reliable source of confidence: the Lord who "is good," whose "mercy endures forever." It is better to "take refuge in the Lord" and in his "steadfast love" than to "put confidence in mortals" or any human achievement. (Read the rest of the *Responsorial Psalm* 118).

If we go to our Father as little children, he will always keep us safe. If we think we have no need of him, we are fools.

Matthew 7:21-27 also speaks of security. Yesterday's focus was food; today's is shelter.

Animals need little more than a place out of the wind to sleep. But humans need structures. We build houses.

It is the same with laws: animals follow the physical laws of their environment. Humans need more structure. But if we just follow the laws, written and unwritten, of our environment, our culture, we are asking for destruction.

Jesus tells us how to build a safe, reliable structure for our lives. "Anyone who hears my words and puts them into practice is like the wise person who built a house on rock." Notice he said "my words," which are much more extensive than his laws.

His words reveal the full will, the heart and mind, of his Father. Our security is to "do the will of our Father in heaven." If we understand this, we will welcome Jesus the Builder: *Blessed is he who comes in the name of the Lord!*

Initiative: Accept the shelter of God's love. Be aware of him always.

First Week of Advent — Friday

December 2, 2011

The Lord is my light and my salvation.
(Responsorial: Psalm 27)

Is our Father just a benevolent tyrant who uses power to enforce good rather than evil? **Isaiah 29:17-24** could give us that impression. When God restores Israel the earthly tyrants will "be no more." The "arrogant" and all "alert to do evil will be cut off." It sounds like God is going to clean them out.

Surprise! The passage ends: "Those who err in spirit shall acquire understanding, and those who find fault shall receive instruction." Our Father is going to convert them.

Our response to evil is "fight or flight." God has another option: light. *The Lord is my light and my salvation.* He saves by teaching, enlightening, converting. "On that day the deaf shall hear the words of a book, and out of gloom and darkness the eyes of the blind shall see."

Our God is a God of mercy and compassion. He shows "steadfast love" to good and bad alike. Jesus reveals him as "almighty God and *Father*."

In **Matthew 9:27-31** Jesus is the one giving light. Two blind men call out to him as "Son of David." He responds as the "Son of the Father," the "reflection of God's glory and the exact imprint of God's very being," who "sustains all things by his powerful word." He enables them to see him by faith.

Jesus is the Word made flesh. His is the day when the deaf shall not just "hear the words of a book," but the deaf and blind together "shall see" the Word of God made flesh before their eyes.

That day is our day. It is the day we look forward to in Advent, but which is already here. Advent just reminds us that the light we are longing for is already in our midst. We only have to open our eyes and receive it. What stops us? It is our lack of faith.

When the blind men called out to him, Jesus asked them: "Are you confident I can do this?" And when, at his touch, they "recovered their sight," he told them it was "because of your faith." We don't see what Jesus wants to show us because we don't really "have confidence" it will do us any good.

Let's be real. How many people read the words of God in Scripture? Do those who don't read really think they are missing anything? They don't have enough faith to believe they are.

How many of the great spiritual books in the Church's two-thousand-year-old library have you read? Why not? How often do you make retreats? Are you in a discussion group?

Could it be you are more blind than the two who met Jesus on the road, but just don't have enough faith to call out to him?

Since you are reading these *Reflections*, the above may be "preaching to the choir." If so, if you have faith and light, hear what Jesus said to Peter: "I have prayed for you that your own faith may not fail.... *strengthen your brothers.*"[1]

---

[1] *Hebrews* 1:3; *John* 1:1-18; *Luke* 22:32.

Initiative: Believe in the light. Read, reflect and share God's words with others.

Saturday First Week of Advent

December 3, 2011

Happy are all who long for the coming of the Lord!
(*Responsorial: Psalm* 147)

The Jews of Jesus' time had only a hazy idea of the afterlife, and a pretty negative one at that. The Sadducees didn't believe in it at all.

So in **Isaiah 30:19-26** God uses material blessings on earth to describe what he will do for his People: abundant food and drink, clear instruction about how to live (see yesterday), good crops, healthy cattle, healing for "wounds" and "bruises."

Except for the instruction—which only a few really listened to, then as now—we know that those material blessings never happened—or didn't last long. And the happiness God was promising through the imagery will not be complete or permanent until "that day" when Jesus returns in glory.

That is what Advent is all about. It is a season when the Church, speaking with the voice of God, calls us to "lift up" our heads and our hearts. To ask ourselves what we really want out of life, now and forever. What we really believe God has promised us. Whether we really have hope he will give it to us. Whether our love is in fact settling for less than the All Good we could love with *all* our heart, soul, and mind.[1]

Notice the repetition of "really." It is easy to be unreal about religion. To think we believe something, even though our faith has no effect on our actions. To take for granted we are hoping for something we aren't doing anything to acquire. To feel confident we love God just because we say we do. The first thing Advent says to us is, "Get real!" *Happy are all who long for the coming of the Lord!* If they really do.

In **Matthew 9:35 to 10:8** Jesus is looking at the effects of unreal religion. The crowds he saw were "harassed and helpless, like sheep without a shepherd." Another translation says "lying prostrate from exhaustion," like those we see today who complain they are "tired to death" of what they are getting from teachers and religious authorities.

Jesus' response was to ask the Father to "send out laborers into his harvest." Laborers who would do what he was doing. First, he "toured all the towns and villages." His workers must *be his body* as *laity* who "in the midst of the world and of secular affairs" *make him present everywhere* as a kind of leaven.[2]

Second, he "taught." His workers must be *disciples* who teach as they *learn*.

Third, he "proclaimed the Good News." To do this credibly, his witnesses must reveal the power of grace in their lifestyle as *prophets*.

Fourth, he "cured every sickness," everything that diminishes "life to the full." His ministers must mediate divine life to others as *priests in the Priest*.

Finally, he "gave them authority" to promote change and reshape society as *stewards of his kingship*.

---

[1] See *Deuteronomy* 6:5; *Matthew* 22:37.
[2] Vatican II, *Apostolate of the Laity*, no. 2.

Initiative: Be Christ. Continue his mission as Prophet, Priest, and King.

FOR REFLECTION AND DISCUSSION: FIRST WEEK OF ADVENT

The Beginning of Religion

The first and basic act of religion is to enter into conscious relationship with God.

Invitation: To focus during Advent and Christmas on *awareness* of my relationship with God as Father.

For prayer and discussion: How many of these statements do you feel you understand? How often are you consciously aware of them?

Sunday: Advent is rich with a double meaning; it focuses on the beginning and the end: the inauguration of Christianity at Christ's birth; the fulfillment of Christianity at the end of the world when he returns in triumph.

The "grace" that Jesus came to give us is the *favor* of *sharing in the divine life of God.* This is why we can call God "*Our Father.*"

When we act in grace, Jesus the Son acts *with us, in us, and through us.* And we act *through him, with him, and in him.* This is to be authentic "children of the Father."

Jesus comes to each of us many times a day, in the form of thoughts, inspirations, challenges. To live "life to the full" we need to be *aware.*

Monday: Because we are "in Christ" by Baptism, we share in the divine life of God. This is the only way we can "know the Father" as the Father he is.

Tuesday: If we find religion burdensome, or do not find comfort in thinking about our Father, we should rethink what we have learned.

Wednesday: For what we believe to find expression in our lives, and make a difference to ourselves and others, we have to be *aware* of it.

Thursday: If our religion doesn't encourage and give us confidence, then either something is wrong with us or wrong with the way we understand our religion.

Friday: Our "knee-jerk" response to evil is "fight or flight." God has another option: light. He saves by teaching, enlightening, converting.

Saturday: Advent is a season when the Church calls us to ask ourselves what we really want out of life.

It is easy to be unreal about religion. To think we believe something, even though our faith has no effect on our actions. Advent says to us, "Get real!"

Initiatives:
Ask seriously: "How can I use the time of Advent to become a happier person?"
Be aware of the face of God as revealed. Read Scripture—daily.
Be aware of your experience of the Father. Go deep in your heart.
Take seriously the gift of faith. Profess it and share it.
Be aware: Notice the table your Father sets before you. Take and eat.
Accept the shelter of God's love. Be aware of him always.
Believe in the light: Read, reflect, and share God's words.
Be Christ: Continue his mission as Prophet, Priest, and King.

Sunday Second Sunday of Advent

December 4, 2011
Discovering the Good News

"Lord, let us see your kindness and grant us your salvation."
(*Responsorial: Psalm* 85)

Inventory

What do you consider good news? What would really "make your day" if it happened right now? Stop. Think of what it is before you read further.

So what did you say? Think about it. How good would that news be? How good will it be a hundred years from now? Will you still be just as excited about it?

Input

A man once asked Jesus: "Good Teacher, what must I do to inherit eternal life?" Jesus answered him, "Why do you call me good? No one is good but God alone."

Why did he say that? What was his point?

We know he was saying that there is a difference between a "good teacher" and the Word of God made flesh; the One of whom the Father said, "This is my Son, the Beloved; listen to him!" Jesus is not like any other. Ultimately, we have only one Teacher. Anything we learn from others, if it does not come from him, has very limited value.[1]

The same is true of news. There is only one Good News: the news that Jesus Christ has come, is coming, and will come. Any other news is a distraction.

So in the *Responsorial* we ask God for the news we want to hear: *"Lord, let us see your kindness and grant us your salvation."*

That is what the readings are all about.

[1] *Mark* 9:7; 10:17; *John* 1:1-18.

Cry Comfort

Isaiah 40:1-11 announces the good news of comfort: "Comfort, give comfort to my people, says your God."

The best news is not what this says about what will happen; it is what it says about God. Our God reveals himself to us as a God who wants to comfort us, a God of love. Jesus will tell us later he is our *Father*. He has made us to be, not only his creatures but his children.

That is more than good news; it is *the* Good News. And it is news about God.

We are glad to hear that our "guilt is expiated" and that things will be well with us. But that is not the real message. The really good news is that "the glory of the Lord shall be revealed, and all the human race shall see it together." When Jesus taught us to pray, he told us to focus first on what God is: "Father in heaven! Hallowed be thy name!"

First we ask, *"Lord, let us see your kindnesss."* Let us know who and what you are. Then we add, *"and grant us your salvation."* We should remember that they go together. Salvation is to "dwell in the house of the Lord" forever, seeing his kindness. We need to focus on his kindness now. "Father in heaven! Hallowed be thy name!"

Just to do that is a foretaste of heaven.

News that Is New:

In **Mark 1:1-8** John the Baptizer is not so much announcing the Good News as announcing that it is going to be announced.

John was "proclaiming a baptism of repentance which led to the forgiveness of sins." If this were all, we could say (with great respect) that it is the "same old same old" we find all through the Old Testament. And (let's be honest) it sounds like what was taught and preached to us all our lives.

If we grew up thinking Christianity was mostly a matter of keeping out of sin—and going to Confession when we failed—we need to listen to the rest of John's message:

> One who is more powerful than I is coming after me; I am not worthy to stoop down and untie his sandal straps.
>
> *I have baptized you with water. He will baptize you in the Holy Spirit.*

Have we heard that? Didn't most of us grow up thinking that the purpose of Baptism was to "take away original sin"? We learned it also gave us "grace," but probably no one ever explained to us very clearly what that meant. To this day most of us would go blank if asked about our experience of being "baptized in the Holy Spirit."

We may not really "know" much more than what John preached. But this is not the Good News Jesus sent his disciples to announce. Before ascending into heaven, he "ordered them not to leave Jerusalem, but to wait there for the promise of the Father," Pentecost:

> For John baptized with water, but you will be baptized with the Holy Spirit not many days from now.

They had to receive the Spirit to preach the Spirit. And without the Spirit there is no Good News. This was how the Apostles knew whether people had really been evangelized:

> Paul came to Ephesus, where he found some disciples. He said to them, "Did you receive the Holy Spirit when you became believers?" They replied, "No, we have not even heard that there is a Holy Spirit." Then he said, "Into what then were you baptized?" They answered, "Into John's baptism."
>
> Paul said, "John baptized with the baptism of repentance, telling the people to believe in the one who was to come after him; that is, in Jesus." On hearing this, they were baptized in the name of the Lord Jesus. When Paul had laid his hands on them, the Holy Spirit came upon them.[1]

What would Paul think of us if we told him about our experience of Baptism? Is it any wonder four popes have called for a "New Evangelization"?

The Good News is that by Baptism we receive the "grace of the Lord Jesus Christ." And that grace cannot be understood outside of the mystery

SUNDAY SECOND SUNDAY OF ADVENT

of "dying" in Christ on the cross and "rising" with him as a "new creation."

We are not children of God because we have repented of our sins. We are sons and daughters of the Father only because we *gave up* the human lives we received at birth, and *gave our bodies to Christ* to be his body. Each of us says with Paul, "I live now, not I, but Christ lives in me." And we live "in him." We are "sons and daughters *in the Son*," which is the only way we can be. "And because we are children, God has sent the Spirit of his Son into our hearts, crying, 'Abba! Father!'"[2]

If we do not know the Father as *our* Father, the way Jesus knows him, how can we know ourselves as sharing truly in the life of the Son? The Church teaches that by Baptism we "became Christ." How can we believe that unless we experience his Father as our Father?[3]

Not to be discouraged. We just have to ask if we have ever really heard the Good News; and if not, John calls us to "make ready" for it. "Clear a straight path" so the mystery can get through.

NEVER TOO LATE

2 Peter 3:8-14 tells that "with the Lord one day is like a thousand years, and a thousand years are like one day." We have to quit measuring; just live in the present moment, doing all we can to bring ourselves and all creation to fulfillment for the "day of the Lord."

If we haven't been evangelized, let's get to it! The New Evangelization is what the American bishops called for, under a different name, when they urged every one of us to make serious *Faith Formation* the first priority in parish, school, and family life.[4]

Formation is not the same as instruction. Real *Faith Formation* is "reiterated instruction combined with insistent intentionality." That means we have to keep learning (or explaining to others) the truth while insisting that we (and others) live it out in *action*. This takes time.

If we are told the same truth often enough, we will eventually hear it. If we think about it long enough, eventually we will begin to understand it. And if we put it into action consistently enough, finally we will experience it.

That is *Faith Formation*. "*Lord, let us see your kindness and grant us your salvation.*"

---

[1] *Acts* 1:4-5; 19:1-6.
[2] *Galatians* 2:20; 4:6.
[3] See *Catechism of the Catholic Church*, no. 795.
[4] *Our Hearts Were Burning Within Us: A Pastoral Plan for Adult Faith Formation in the United States* (USCCB), November 17, 1999 is available in print by telephoning (800) 235-8722. Ask for publication number 5-299 for the English edition or 5-811 for Spanish.

INSIGHT
What difference is there—in experience, not theory— between the baptism of John and that of Jesus? Which is closer to my experience?

INITIATIVE
Use Advent to begin a serious plan of Faith Formation. Choose your first step.

Second Week of Advent — Monday

December 5, 2011

Our God will come to save us!
(*Responsorial: Psalm* 85, *Isaiah* 35:4)

Isaiah 35:1-10 promises: "a highway...called the Holy Way.... It is for those with a journey to make, and on it the redeemed shall walk."

A foundational element of the spiritual life is just to be *aware* that we have "a journey to make." That we need to be going somewhere in our relationship with God, with other people, with the world. If we are not growing, we are stagnating.

To entice us, God tells us what we will see: "The parched land... will bloom with abundant flowers and rejoice with joyful song," But it is not only human beauty: "They will see the glory of the Lord, the splendor of our God."

Not just in heaven. Here and now. Jesus promises "life to the full" here and hereafter. And we don't have to be "good enough" to "achieve" it. Just be open enough to the promise: *Our God will come to save us!*

To make this personal, ask, "Do I believe this? Do I really believe that if I embark on a 'journey' into deeper knowledge and love of God, he will reveal himself to me? That I will see beauty, and experience goodness, greater than what anything on earth, anything merely created, can give me?"

Do I think this is only for "saints," not for mediocre people like myself? God says to "those with a fearful heart":

> Be strong, do not fear! Here is your God... He will come and save you.

Then the eyes of the blind shall be opened, and the ears of the deaf unstopped; the lame shall leap like a deer, and the tongue of the speechless sing for joy.

God is giving you your existence right now, and all you can do with it. God is giving you his own divine life, so that, in union with him, you can do what God does. You don't need strength; you just need to believe. And trust. And choose to desire, which is love.

Do you?

The "Holy Way" is simple. Jesus outlined it in the "*Our Father*," *whose first five phrases are five phases of spiritual growth*. Sublime but simple, challenging but easy. It is "for those with a journey to make." Do you choose to be one of them?[1]

In **Luke 5:17-26**, "some men came to Jesus, carrying a paralyzed man on a mat." Note that the man was paralyzed. Not just weak. Not unwilling to walk. He was paralyzed, *unable* to walk.

Spiritually, are you worse off than he was? Do you think you are unable to travel the Holy Way? Too sinful? Not special enough to God?

The first thing Jesus did was call the paralyzed man his "friend." Then he said, "Your sins are forgiven." End of problem. Then he said, "Get up and walk!" *Our God will come to save us!*

So why not just do it?

---

[1] For more detailed instruction, refer to pages 3-11 of this booklet.

Initiative: Make the first step. Believe *our God will come to save us!*

Tuesday Second Week of Advent

December 6, 2011

The Lord our God comes in strength!
(*Responsorial: Psalm* 96, *Isaiah* 40:9-10)

In **Isaiah 40:1-11,** when God proclaims "Comfort, O comfort my people," he follows it with, "Prepare the way of the Lord. Make straight... a highway for our God." He comforts through leadership. There is comfort just in knowing you are going somewhere.

We can find comfort in just being; especially if we are aware of being held by God, sustained in existence, and protected by our Father. *Psalm* 131 speaks of being "in quiet and silence, like a child in its mother's arms." But often even this includes being rocked.

What is not comforting is stagnation. Or the idleness that is not repose from labor but just "hanging around." We feel the world-weariness Christopher Fry captures in *Sleep of Prisoners*:

> We lean on our lives
> Expecting destiny to keep her date...
> Ah, it's a long waste of breath....

So God comes with a road-building project to wake up the world! *The Lord our God comes in strength!*

> Every valley shall be filled in, every mountain and hill be made low; the rugged ground shall be made a plain, the rough country, a broad valley.

Then "the glory of the Lord shall be revealed, and all people shall see it together." But only if they get moving. You can't expect to see the "glory of God" if all you do is go to church on Sunday and go home. Isaiah said yesterday that the Holy Way "is for those with a journey to make, and on it the redeemed shall walk." If you are not bent on forward motion, you can wonder just how redeemed you are.

The key question is: "Am I aware of my religion, my spiritual life as a journey? Is there a point I am trying to reach? Am I clear about how to get there?" If the answer to any of these is "No," you are like the crowds Jesus looked out on: "lying prostrate... like sheep without a shepherd." Getting nowhere.

In **Matthew 18:12-14** Jesus tells us how his Father feels about this. We could have guessed it already from what Jesus said about himself: "I came that they might have life, and *have it to the full*!" The Father, the Son, and the Spirit all live life to the full, and want to share it with us. Jesus designed the Church to be a hotbed of energy, enlightenment, and growth. Those who wander away from the flock, who no longer assemble to be fed or led to greener pastures, are "strays." Jesus worries about them.

But there is no point in bringing them back to the flock if the flock itself is just "lying around like sheep without a shepherd." There has to be leadership. Someone—whether clergy or lay—has to know the way. And point it out. "Go up onto a high mountain... Cry out at the top of your voice... Here is your God!" *The Lord our God comes in strength!*

For those without the will to grow, there is simply "no way." But where there is a will, the "five phrases" of the *Our Father* show five phases of the way.

Initiative: Make a choice, "To grow or not to grow." Think of the alternative.

SECOND WEEK OF ADVENT — WEDNESDAY

DECEMBER 7, 2011

O bless the Lord, my soul!
(Responsorial: Psalm 103)

Isaiah 40:25-31 gives the basis for authentic *Fear of the Lord*. This is the divine gift of *perspective*—the "Gift of the Holy Spirit" Scripture calls the "beginning of Wisdom."[1]

Fear without the emotion of fright is simply *perspective*. God says in *Isaiah*, "To whom can you liken me as an equal?" And he suggests that, in order to understand who he is, we "lift up our eyes" to the heavens, look at the stars and ask, "Who has created these things?" God is the One who

> leads out their army and numbers them, calling them all by name! By his great might and the strength of his power none of them is missing.

We know, although Isaiah didn't, that:

> our earth is just a tiny planet in a vast Solar System. And our Solar System is just one member of a vast Milky Way galaxy with *200 to 400 billion stars*.... The most current estimates guess that there are *100 to 200 billion galaxies in the Universe*, each of which has hundreds of billions of stars.[2]

And we don't know how many Universes there might be. Does that put God in perspective for us?

So "the Lord is the eternal God, creator of the ends of the earth." And what does he do with his power? "He gives strength to the fainting; for the weak he makes vigor abound."

> They that hope in the LORD will renew their strength, they will soar as with eagles' wings. They will run and not grow weary, walk and not grow faint.

Understood this way, does *Fear of the Lord* give us reason to say: "O bless the Lord, my soul; and all my being, bless his holy name!" Does it give us new appreciation of our *Father*?[3]

And does it encourage us to join those who follow "the Holy Way," those who are aware they have "a journey to make"? Does it give us a reason to look closely at the "five phases" of the journey in the first "five phrases" of the prayer Jesus taught us?

In **Matthew 11:28-30** Jesus takes away any remaining fright that *Fear of the Lord* may arouse in us: "Come to me, all you who are weary and find life burdensome, and I will refresh you." If any still think of "religion" as a "burden, hard to bear," this does not come from exposure to the mind and heart of God! Jesus says:

> The scribes and the Pharisees sit on Moses' seat; therefore, do whatever they teach you and follow it; but do not do as they do.... They tie up heavy burdens, hard to bear, and lay them on the shoulders of others....

He tells us how to follow his Way:

> Take my yoke upon you, and learn from me; for I am gentle and humble in heart, and you will find rest for your souls. For my yoke is easy, and my burden is light.

---

[1] *Isaiah* 11:1-2; *Psalm* 111:10; *Proverbs* 1:7; 9:10; *Catechism of the Catholic Church* 1831.
[2] Google www.universetoday.com.
[3] Read the rest of *Psalm* 103. See *Exodus* 3:13-14; *Psalms* 139, 147.

Initiative: Convert fear into *Fear of the Lord*. Say *bless the Lord, my soul!*

THURSDAY THE IMMACULATE CONCEPTION

DECEMBER 8, 2011
The Immaculate Conception of the Blessed Virgin Mary

Sing to the Lord a new song, for he has done marvelous deeds.
(*Responsorial: Psalm* 98)

The readings are about lifting up our eyes to God "who has blessed us in Christ with every spiritual blessing," not just "in the heavens," but beyond the scope of our dreams.

INVENTORY

Does it impress you that "in the heavens" there are 100 to 200 *billion* galaxies in the Universe, each of which has a hundred billion stars? What if we factor in the dimension of *time*? Astronomers calculate, using different formulae, that our universe is between 11 and 18 billion years old. Humans have existed as a genus for only a fraction of that time. And all that is nothing compared to the time the "eternal Lord" has been around! Let's look at *distance*:

> The closest star to Earth is the Sun... located about 150 million kilometers away. Light alone takes 8 minutes to travel from the Sun to the Earth. If you were to make a road trip to the Sun, traveling at an average speed of 120 kilometers per hour, it would take you about 1.25 million hours to drive there; that's 143 years....
>
> The nearest star to the Sun is Proxima Centauri, located about 4.2 light years away. In other words, light alone takes 4.2 years to make the 40 trillion kilometer journey to Proxima Centauri.... A spaceship (moving at the fastest current speed of 70,000 kilometers per hour) would need about 65,000 years to reach the nearest star.
>
> And Proxima Centauri is a really close star! The most distant star you can see without a telescope is about 5,000 light years away. The center of the Milky Way is about 26,000 light years away, and the nearest large galaxy (which you can see with the unaided eye) is Andromeda, located about 2.5 million light years away.

In other words, even if we developed spaceships traveling at the speed of light, there are stars visible to the naked eye that no passenger could live long enough to reach.[1]

What is "in the heavens" is impressive. Are you keenly aware that it does not even compare in impressiveness with the reality the Church celebrates today?

INPUT

The alternative *Opening Prayer* tells us "the image of the Virgin is found in the Church." And vice-versa, Mary is the image of the Church. The first devotional title given her was "Mirror of the Church." In her we see ourselves as we will be when Christ "presents the Church to himself in splendor... holy and without blemish." The *Preface* calls her "our pattern of holiness," God's "sign of favor to the Church in its beginning and the *promise of its perfection* as the bride of Christ, radiant in beauty."

The *Preface* for the feast of the Assumption, sees in her "the "pattern of the Church in its perfection." What Mary was from the beginning of her life, we will be at the end of ours. Her Immaculate Conception is the preview and

THE IMMACULATE CONCEPTION — THURSDAY

promise of our "immaculate conclusion." At the end, Jesus, who has conquered sin and death, will make us "perfect, as our heavenly Father is perfect."[2] That is something to make "creating the heavens" look like child's play!

[1] See National Aeronautics and Space Administration, http://map.gsfc.nasa.gov; http://www.universetoday.com; http://earthguide.ucsd.edu.
[2] *Ephesians* 5:27; *Matthew* 5:48.

ONE TO ALL, ALL TO ONE

Once you've created one star, letting it multiply into a few billion more is a ho-hummer. But if people's sins multiply into the billions, it goes beyond imagination to say God can draw them all together and annihilate them in one "*perfect man* who is *Christ come to full stature.*" That is the work God began when he arranged that Mary should be conceived in her mother's womb without coming under the power of sin. When Christ, the "fruit of her womb," hung on the cross, all the billions of sins throughout the history of the world were condensed into one body, taken down to the grave, and annihilated. He is the "Lamb of God who *takes away* the sins of the world."

Genesis 3:9-20 tells us in story form how sin began. Paul described it later:

> Sin came into the world through one man, and death came through sin, and so death spread to all because all have sinned.[1]

Mary's was the first human body to be conceived immune from the "power of sin," from which no human being born to be raised, formed, programmed, and conditioned by a culture infected by the sins of many, is exempt.

She was exempt, not for her own sake, but so that the body of Jesus, the Word made flesh of her flesh, would never have been under the power of sin. And we, through incorporation into that body over which sin could have no power, are purified of our sins by identification with him, dying and rising "in him" in the mystery of redemption. *Sing to the Lord a new song, for he has done marvelous deeds!*

BLESSED IN CHRIST

Ephesians 1:3-12 spells out what it means to say God "has blessed us with every spiritual blessing in the heavens."

> He chose us in Christ before the foundation of the world to be holy and blameless before him in love. He destined us for adoption as his children....

The power to preserve is the power to restore. What Mary was totally and absolutely preserved from, we will be totally and absolutely freed from. Through dying and rising in Christ at Baptism, we were purified of all sin, to be "without a spot or wrinkle or anything of the kind... holy and without blemish" when we are presented to Jesus at the "marriage supper of the Lamb." *Sing to the Lord a new song, for he has done marvelous deeds!* But none more marvelous than that.[2]

The God who revealed his love like this is the God we are speaking of when we say, *"Our Father, who art in heaven...."* We need to foster *awareness* of that.

A GROUND-LEVEL EVENT

To understand **Luke 1:26-38** imagine yourself outside on a clear night filled

THURSDAY THE IMMACULATE CONCEPTION

with stars. As you look at the immensity of the universe, you see what seems to be a star brighter than all the others coming into your range of vision from far beyond all you can see. It is moving, falling toward earth, getting bigger and bigger, brighter and brighter as it comes.

You are fascinated. You feel you could watch it forever.

Finally, you see it reach earth, far in the distance. You have no way of knowing how far. You expect an explosion, but there is none; just a bright, huge glow that pulses once, then recedes into itself and disappears.

You wonder. Then, moved by an impulse you have never had before, you set out to find it.

You travel two, three years, always asking people to point to where they saw the light come to earth. Finally you reach a place where the people point back in the direction you came from. You know you have arrived.

You retrace your steps to a small village. The people there say, "Yes, the light came down here. We expected to be annihilated. But there was nothing but the light and an exhilarating warmth. It surrounded that house over there, pulsed once, then just fell back into itself and disappeared."

You go to the house. It belongs to a man named Joachim and his wife Anne. They say, "Yes, there was a light, but we don't know what it was all about. It filled the house for a moment with an indescribable warmth and joy, then seemed to recede into our daughter Mary, who was sitting there. Then things went back to normal."

You ask, "What did your daughter say about it? Was she different after that?"

"Not really. Well, yes, she seemed more—'recollected' is the word I think the rabbis use. She just seemed more *aware*, and more filled with peace and happiness than before. But you have to understand, she was always an extremely peaceful, happy girl. She just became more so, that's all."

"She didn't say anything at all when it happened?"

"Well, yes, but she never explained it. After the light seemed to enter into her and be swallowed up, as it were, she just repeated a few times, so softly we could hardly hear her, "Let it be with me according to your word."

"*Sing to the Lord a new song, for he has done marvelous deeds.*"

[1] *Romans* 5:12.
[2] *Revelation* 9:19.

INSIGHT
Do I understand the immensity of what happened at Mary's Immaculate Conception? Do I see what this says about me?

INITIATIVE
Say to God, "Let it be with me according to your word." Then be what you are.

Second Week of Advent — Friday

December 9, 2011

Those who follow you, Lord, will have the light of life.
(*Responsorial: Psalm 1*)

Why would anyone who hears what God says in **Isaiah 48:17-19** not try to do everything God says? "I, the LORD your God, teach you what is *for your own good*." Do we just not believe it?

> If you would hearken to my commandments, your prosperity would be like a river, and your success like the waves of the sea... Your descendants would be like the sand.... Their name never cut off or blotted out from my presence.

It has to be that we just don't believe that living the way God teaches will make us truly happy. If we don't give time to reading and reflecting on his words, trying to put them into action, we simply cannot say sincerely: *Those who follow you, Lord, will have the light of life*. So what light do we believe in?

Scary as it is to say it, the answer is "our own." The Capital Sin of *Pride* is defined as making oneself the *criterion* of truth and falsehood, good and evil. Few people are stupid enough to claim this in theory. They would not say it in words. But in practice, it is the principle many live by. They say it in actions.

Everyone follows some guidance system, whether they can identify it or not. If I have in practice rejected God's way (by just not trying to learn and understand it deeply), then I am probably following the current ideals and values of my culture. But if I do not accept to see myself as simply a conformist, most likely I have decided—unconsciously, perhaps—just to accept what I myself think is true and to follow what I feel is good. The definition of this is the "Capital Sin" of *Pride*. I have made myself the criterion.

We have to "follow our conscience," of course. But unless we are blinded by *Pride* we will feel conscience-bound to seek enlightenment from God. And unless we renounce the faith, we will look for his light in the Church.

If we renounce the truth embodied in the words of God, this is about as scary as things get. No one is the criterion but God. When I make myself God I am choosing darkness and death.

In **Matthew 11:16-19** Jesus challenges those who say they do not go to church because of the priest or congregation. People rejected Jesus himself because they didn't think he was austere enough in lifestyle or strict enough in ministry: "The Son of Man appeared eating and drinking, and they say, 'This one is a glutton and drunkard, a lover of... those outside the law.'" But "John appeared neither eating nor drinking, and people say, 'He is mad!'" Those who drop out of the Church do not leave because of the messengers. Messengers come in all shapes and sizes. They leave because they don't want to hear the message. It is Jesus, not his ministers, they are rejecting. "Whoever listens to you listens to me, and whoever rejects you rejects me." That goes to the heart of the matter. The root sin is *Pride*.

Initiative: Be peaceful with the truth that you need to seek enlightenment from God. Look for it in his words and in the teaching based on them.

Saturday Second Week of Advent

December 10, 2011

Lord, make us turn to you. Let us see your face and we shall be saved.
(Responsorial: Psalm 80)

Why do we ask God to "make us" turn to him? We know he will not force our free wills. And we saw yesterday that people reject the message whether the messengers seem strict or gentle, austere or approachable. No matter how God appeals to us, we can ignore him.

Sirach 48:1-11 shows God using "strong-arm tactics." Elijah was a very tough prophet. He got people's attention by cutting off the food supply. He "shut up the heavens" by drought. He "brought down fire" from heaven to kill soldiers and expose false prophets. If anyone could put the "fear of the Lord" into people, it was Elijah. Except that life-giving *Fear of the Lord* is a Gift of the Holy Spirit, and displays of power as such cannot produce it.[1]

Still, in Elijah, God used fright for a loving purpose: to "turn the hearts of parents to their children, and the disobedient to the wisdom of the righteous, to make ready a people prepared for the Lord." God our Father, in his love, will do whatever he can to save us from our blindness and self-destructiveness. But when Jesus came, the time for strong-arm tactics was over.

In **Matthew 17:9-13**, Jesus responded to a Jewish tradition that Elijah was going to return before the Messiah came. He told his disciples, "Elijah has already come" in the person of John the Baptizer. Before John's birth the angel applied to him the prophecy that Elijah would "turn the hearts" of people back to God, their true Father.[2]

But unlike Elijah, John, in spite of his awesome lifestyle and strong denunciations of Herod, the Sadducees and Pharisees, did not use force. On the contrary, he was delivered up to his enemies and killed.[3]

In this he was the "precursor," the one who "ran before" the Messiah, in a way that made him more than a messenger. Jesus said his deliverance into the hands of his enemies was a preview of what God would allow to happen to Jesus himself: "The Son of Man will suffer at their hands in the same way."

This is a change of tactics. God appeals to us now through the witness of weakness rather than force. Instead of killing to show us his power, he will die to show us his love.

Both ways were acts of love. But to our eyes weakness is less ambiguous. The *Fear of the Lord* that comes from the revelation of God's awesome love in the Jesus who gave himself up to death for us has no fright in it at all. What we see in *perspective* is not the difference between our *power* and God's, but between our *love* and the love of God which "surpasses all understanding."

Jesus came to "turn back the hearts" of children who lived in fear of their Father by revealing the Father's love embodied in the Son. *"Lord, make us turn to you."*

[1] *1 Kings* 17:1; 18:36-40; 21:19; *2 Kings* 1:9-14, 17.
[2] *Luke* 1:13-17.
[3] *Matthew* 3:7; 11:2-5; *Mark* 6:17-18.

Initiative: Live in awe, not just of God's power, but of his love.

FOR REFLECTION AND DISCUSSION: SECOND WEEK OF ADVENT

Discovering the Good News

There is only one Good News: The news that Jesus Christ has come, is coming, and will come. Any other news is a distraction.

Invitation: To embrace the Father's kindness in giving us salvation.

For prayer and discussion: How many of these statements do you feel you understand? How often are you consciously aware of them?

Sunday: Our God reveals himself to us as God who wants to comfort us, a God of love. Jesus will tell us later he is our *Father*. He has made us to be not only his creatures but his children. That is more than good news; it is *the* Good News. And it is news about God.

If we do not know the Father as *our* Father, the way Jesus knows him, how can we know ourselves as sharing truly in the life of the Son? The Church teaches that by Baptism we "became Christ." How can we believe that unless we experience his Father as our Father?

Monday: A foundational element of the spiritual life is just to be *aware* that we have "a journey to make."

Tuesday: The Father, Son, and Spirit live life to the full, and want to share it with us. Jesus designed the Church to be a hotbed of energy, enlightenment, and growth.

Wednesday: …authentic *Fear of the Lord*…. is the divine gift of *perspective*. It is the "Gift of the Holy Spirit" that Scripture calls the "beginning of Wisdom."

Fear without the emotion of fright is simply *perspective*.

Thursday: The power to preserve is the power to restore. What Mary was totally and absolutely preserved from, we will be totally and absolutely freed from.

Friday: Why would anyone who hears what God says in Isaiah 48:17-19 not try to do everything God says? "I, the LORD…teach you what is *for your own good*."

Saturday: Jesus came to "turn back the hearts" of children who lived in fear of their Father by revealing the Father's love embodied in the Son.

Initiatives:
Use Advent to begin a serious plan of Faith Formation. Choose your first step.
Make the first step. Believe *our God will come to save us!*
Make a choice: "To grow or not to grow." Think of the alternative.
Convert fear into *Fear of the Lord*. Say, *"Bless the Lord, my soul!"*
Say to God, "Let it be with me according to your word." Then be what you are.
Recognize the mystery of who you are. Keep yourself aware of it.
Be peaceful with the truth that you need to seek enlightenment from God. Look for it in his words and in the teaching based on them.
Live in awe, not just of God's power, but of his love.

Sunday   Third Sunday of Advent

December 11, 2011
Jesus Saves Us From Sin

My soul rejoices in my God.
(Responsorial: Isaiah 61:10)

Inventory

What does hope have to do with joy? What role does hope play in the "joy of salvation"? What do you hope for from God? How do you expect God to fulfill that hope?

Input

The *Entrance Antiphon* tells us we should *always* rejoice—even when things are going wrong and we are suffering: "Rejoice in the Lord always!" And the reason given is because "the Lord is near." Obviously the Scripture is telling us that if the Lord is with us, nothing can really harm us. No matter how sad we feel, we know in our hearts that if Jesus is with us and within us we have everything we need for the fullness of joy—forever, if we keep ourselves *aware* of it.

The *Opening Prayer* asks that we may "*experience* the joy of salvation." This is hard if we only focus on what is bad in the world. So we need to look at what God is doing. In Advent the Church urges us to "look forward to the birthday of Christ" and "*celebrate* it with love and thanksgiving." This is not hard to do, but if we neglect to do it we will not *experience* the joy of Christmas or of salvation as we should. Awareness is the site of faith-experience. We need to cultivate it.

We "look forward" to Christ's coming—whether at Christmas or at the end of the world—first, by *calling it into memory*. We use material, visible, audible things to keep us aware of what is going to happen: Advent wreaths, candles, the Bible, special church services, and personal or family prayers, all the visible preparations for Christmas—and all the commercial advertisements that, even when distorted, call us to remember what Christmas is and that Advent is a time we should use to prepare our hearts for it.

Secondly, we "look forward" by *thinking* of what Christ's coming has done, is doing in the world now, and will have done by the time this world ends.

And finally, we "look forward" just by *longing* for "the joy of salvation": spending time consciously letting our hearts go out in desire for knowledge of Jesus, intimate friendship with him, purification from all selfish or disordered desires. Being aware.

God Has Sent Us

The *Responsorial Verse* (Isaiah 61:10) is a summons to joy: "*My soul rejoices in my God.*" We are rejoicing in what the Lord has called and empowered us to do.

In **Isaiah 61:1-11** the prophet is rejoicing because he knows "the spirit of

Third Sunday of Advent — Sunday

the Lord God is upon me," because "he has anointed me," and because "he has sent me." What God has sent him to announce is good news. And that God has anointed and sent him is also good news.

Do I rejoice in the fact that God has anointed me as truly as he anointed Isaiah? At Baptism the minister anointed me with chrism on the top of my head with the words, "As Christ was anointed Priest, Prophet and King, so live always as a member of his body." By this anointing God himself anointed and made me a *prophet*, a *priest,* and a *steward* of the kingship of Christ.

And he *sent* me. Jesus said to his disciples, "As the Father has sent me, so I send you" (*John* 20:21). We are all sent as truly as Isaiah was, and to do essentially the same thing: to announce the good news of Jesus. "Go therefore and make disciples of all nations … And remember, *I am with you always*" (*Matthew* 28:19-20).

Isaiah had personal experience of the good news he announced: "I will greatly rejoice in the LORD... For he has clothed me with the garments of salvation, he has covered me with the robe of righteousness, as a bridegroom decks himself with a garland, and as a bride adorns herself with her jewels." To convince others that Jesus is good news we have to experience him as good news in our own lives. We have to be able to say truthfully, "In my God is the joy of my soul."

How does Jesus "heal me" when I am "brokenhearted"? How does he "proclaim liberty" to me when I feel imprisoned by circumstances or a slave to fears and drives within me? Advent is a time to get in touch with the answers to these questions.

One Among You

Does this mean we have to be "holy" to bring others into contact with Jesus? Not if we think "holy" means "without sin." The good news is that we are "holy" because of what God does and is doing to us; not because of what we do. Being "children of the Father" makes us holy.

In **John 1:6-28** people thought John the Baptizer was holy because of his austere life; they even took him for the Messiah. John said they didn't have a clue! "There is one among you whom you do not recognize… the strap of whose sandal I am not worthy to unfasten." The good news is that *Jesus* is here, *Jesus* is at work, *Jesus* is saving us, *Jesus* has made and is making us holy.

To be "holy" means to be "set apart" by God, chosen, blessed, sanctified by the gift—the pure gift—of his "sanctifying grace," the favor of *sharing in the life of God*.

We don't earn this gift. It is not given to us because we deserve it. It is not proportionate to how well we behave. God has loved us and made us his children, and we are equally loved—equally, undeniably, and irrevocably his children whether we behave well or badly. Grace is a gift and a fact; a rock-bottom reality to rejoice in.

Can we lose it by "mortal sin"? Yes. But if you have you are "dead" to loving God and very unlikely to be bothering to read these words! At least you are not reading them with desire. Mortal sin is not what makes us *feel* "unholy."

SUNDAY THIRD SUNDAY OF ADVENT

When we feel that, it probably means we love God and are very conscious that we ought to love him more. That is a "call sign" of grace.

When we feel bad about our sins we should rejoice that God has given us the gift to feel bad about them! We cannot look down on anything until something in us has risen above it. If we look down on our sins, God has elevated our soul to his level of values. If we recognize the action of grace in us, we will "recognize Jesus" for who he is and what he does. Then we will rejoice, not in our good behavior, but in the gift of God's love: *"My soul rejoices in my God."*

THERE IS ONE WITHIN

In **1 Thessalonians 5:16-24** Paul urges us to stay in touch with the empowering Spirit of God within us. To "rejoice always," he says, "never cease praying; give constant thanks." Rejoice in—and be aware of—the presence of God in your heart. Let his life inspire and guide you, animate you and empower you. "Do not stifle the Spirit."

He tells us to avoid evil, not by focusing on evil, but by focusing on what we are, being aware of what the gift of sharing in God's divine life has made us.

For you are all children of light and… of the day… not of the night or of darkness. So then let us not fall asleep… but… keep awake and be sober.… Since we belong to the day, let us be sober, and put on the breastplate of faith and love, and for a helmet the hope of salvation (*1 Thessalonians* 5-8).

Our defenses are *within* us: faith, and love, and hope. If we are "children of the day" we do the things of daytime. We stay awake, alert to the life of God within us. We walk by his light and power in our hearts.

The Christian life is a life of letting ourselves be empowered—lifted up, enlightened, and loved—by Jesus Christ who is always with us and within us, saving us, setting us apart, and sanctifying us, making us "holy" by sharing his divine life with us. This is the good news: the gift and presence, the goodness and power of Jesus who joins us to himself. *"My soul rejoices in my God."*

Father, enfold me,
Logos, enlighten me,
Spirit uphold me,
Life from above!
Sweet Mary, mother me,
All who are family,
Sister and brother me,
Teach me to love!

INSIGHT
How do I feel when I think of Christ's love? How do I feel when I don't?

INITIATIVE
During Advent form the habit of touching your heart frequently during the day and saying the WIT prayer: "Lord, live with me; live in me; live through me."

Our Lady of Guadalupe — Monday

December 12, 2011

The Almighty has done great things for me, and holy is his name.
(Responsorial: Luke 1:49)

Zechariah 2:14-17 proclaims the source and the consequences of the phrase we use so often at Mass: "The Lord [be] with you!" And this is what the appearance of Our Lady of Guadalupe says to us. When Mary, who is called the "Mirror of the Church," appeared as an Aztec woman, this said to the people of Latin America that the God the Christians proclaimed was not some foreign god of the Spaniards, but "God with you." God in Jesus, born of a woman with the face of all peoples, is "God with you," God one of you, making you one with him.[1]

> Rejoice, O daughter Zion! For I will come and dwell in your midst, says the Lord.

Until Mary appeared, giving the Church a native face, there were very few conversions. After her appearance became known, within seven years eight million Aztecs joined the Church.

> Many nations shall join themselves to the Lord on that day, and shall be my people. I will dwell in your midst. And you shall know that the Lord… has sent me to you.

Today, when millions are leaving a Church perceived as irrelevant, every Christian is called to be a "new apparition" of Our Lady of Guadalupe through a *discerning lifestyle* that reveals the true mystery of the Church—"The Lord with you"—shining through "the good, the true, and the beautiful" in our culture.

> The Lord … will again choose Jerusalem.… For he has roused himself from his holy dwelling.

"The Lord with you" is the source of the Church's life. The more we are *aware* of his presence in us, the more we will *evangelize* by showing the face of Christ in our own milieu.

We find it hard to believe that Christ's face, which is the true face of the Church, can appear in us. In **Luke 1:26-38** Mary had the same problem.

> The angel Gabriel … came to her and said, "Greetings, favored one! The Lord is with you." But she was much perplexed by his words and pondered what sort of greeting this might be.

But what the angel said to her, God's Spirit says now to all who have received the divine life of God at Baptism. To all who have "presented our bodies as a living sacrifice to God" to be the body of Christ on earth he says:

> Do not be afraid… for you have found favor with God…. The Holy Spirit will come upon you, and the power of the Most High will overshadow you; therefore the [fruit of your life] will be holy…. For nothing will be impossible with God.[2]

We just have to believe in the mystery of our Baptism: that we have "become Christ," and "in him" true sons and daughters of the Father. And keep ourselves aware of it, saying all day:

"Here am I, the servant of the Lord; let it be with me according to your word."

---

[1] *Dominus vobiscum.* The "be" is an insertion.
[2] See *Romans* 12:1-2.

Response: Believe and be aware that God is "with you." Let him act in you.

TUESDAY THIRD WEEK OF ADVENT

DECEMBER 13, 2011

The Lord hears the cry of the poor.
(*Responsorial: Psalm* 34)

Scripture consistently keeps us aware that we should *hear the cry of the poor*. **Zephaniah 3:1-13** foretells doom first for those who do not hear the cry of the poverty in their own hearts:

> Woe to the soiled, defiled, oppressing city! She hears no voice; accepts no correction. She has not trusted in the LORD; she has not drawn near to her God.

This is not a description of the "poor in spirit"! Those who are not humbly aware of their own inadequacy and sin cannot hear God's voice, accept his correction, put trust in the Lord or draw near to God. There are no exemptions.

But if we *listen to the cry of the poor*, letting ourselves be aware of the poverty within us and outside of us, we need not fear. Our sins will be forgiven.

> I will remove from your midst your proudly exultant ones, and you shall no longer be haughty.... For I will leave in the midst of you a people humble and lowly. They shall seek refuge in the name of the LORD.

The spirit in our day that this reading condemns is called *triumphalism*. This, along with *clericalism* and *legalism*, was one of the three characteristics of the Curia-drawn agenda that the bishops rejected at the outset of Vatican II. At the time it meant a compulsion to portray the Church as universally triumphing, here and now, over sin and evil, especially in the public image and pronouncements of those members of the hierarchy whom one agrees with. Triumphalists delight in seeing the Pope and cardinals "on display' in the splendor of magnificent robes and ceremony. The triumphalist image is the opposite of the "pilgrim Church" image adopted by the bishops who in Vatican II accepted blame for the "rise of atheism" fed by false or careless teaching of Catholic doctrine.[1]

In truth, the Church *is* triumphing over sin and evil in every age—but as Jesus did on the cross, when the ugliness of him who was "made to be sin" for us was much more visible than his glory. Any other image falsifies the reality.[2]

Matthew 21:28-32 gives an example of the triumphalist spirit in the self-image of those who think they are serving God by publicly professing (and even giving) obedience to laws and legal observances of lesser importance, while ignoring Christ's essential command: "Love one another as I have loved you." They pride themselves on clinging to the simplistic, misunderstood, and often misrepresented teachings of their childhood while rejecting the Church's officially declared doctrinal corrections and reflective new insights. The elder son saw himself as so obedient that once he said, "Yes," he thought no more about it. The younger son was aware of the "No" in his heart and overcame it.

---

[1] See the *Constitution on the Church*, chapter VII; *The Church in the Modern World*, no. 19. Those who Google "triumphalism" will see it has different meanings for different people, but what they all have in common is a narrow sense of superiority based on false or superficial grounds.
[2] *2 Corinthians* 5:21.

Initiative: Be aware of the "No" in you at war with the "Yes" you say to God.

Third Week of Advent WEDNESDAY

December 14, 2011

Let the clouds rain down the Just One, and the earth bring forth a Savior.
(*Responsorial: Psalm* 85)

Isaiah 45:6-25 says some wonderful things about God. Comforting things. Life-giving things. But what good does it do us to hear these things, or to know them, both intellectually and by faith, if we are not *aware* of them?

People who fight may know they love each other; but if, in the heat of anger they are not aware of it, it doesn't prevent cruel words or hurtful actions.

In the *Responsorial* we ask the clouds to *"rain down"* the Just One, and the earth to *"bring forth"* a Savior. We want our God and Savior near, present to us. If not present to our senses, then present in our *awareness* of what we have seen and heard.

St. Catherine of Sienna says that through *memory* we are like God the Father: We say, "Let it be!" and it is.

Three times Isaiah repeats: "I am the Lord, there is no other." Four if we count, "There is no just and saving God but me." To be constantly aware of this is to live in the sense of perspective given by *Fear of the Lord*.

Isaiah makes clear this is fear without fright; that it is the clarity, plus the assurance, given by *perspective*. The God we know and worship, "creator of the heavens, designer and maker of the earth," is a "just and saving God." He says, "Turn to me and be safe." All of his power, all that he wills, is dedicated to our good.

It is when we forget this, when we are not aware of it, that we lose the relationship with God in which alone we find "light," "justice," safety, meaning in life, assurance, inspiration, the fullness of love.

It is to foster this awareness that we pray, read God's words, reflect on them, celebrate what we believe, assemble in the light of faith with others to praise and worship him. And the "source and summit" of all we believe is made present to us at Mass. Jesus said, "Do this in *memory* of me."

We sometimes have difficulty remaining aware of God's goodness. Or retaining clarity about his true character: his mind, will, and intentions toward us.

In **Luke 7:18-23** John the Baptizer himself was tempted to call into question the nature of his relationship with Jesus. He did not understand how Jesus, the Messiah, could leave John, his precursor, abandoned in prison. He sent Jesus a poignant message: "Are you the one who is to come, or not? Should we start looking for someone else?"

Haven't we all felt this at times? Hasn't Jesus disappointed us in our expectations of him?

Jesus answered by telling John to look at what he was doing, not at what he wasn't: "Go and tell John what you have seen and heard: the blind recover their sight, cripples walk... And blessed is anyone who finds no stumbling-block in me." If we remain aware of what God is and has done, we will be able to trust.

Initiative: Remain aware of what you have "seen and heard." Keep the faith.

THURSDAY THIRD WEEK OF ADVENT

DECEMBER 15, 2011

I will praise you, Lord, for you have rescued me.
(*Responsorial: Psalm* 30)

God doesn't keep bad things from happening to us. God made people free, and if they choose to sin they can cause terrible pain to others. And we can diminish—or even destroy—our own lives by our free choices. God has to allow this: freedom is freedom; we can use it or abuse it. But when we do abuse it, or others abuse it and hurt us, God rescues us.

Isaiah 54:1-10 promises Israel (1-4) that a fruitless existence can become fruitful, a hemmed-in life can expand, and the mistakes and shame of the past can be forgotten. Why? Because God is like a husband: he will never abandon Israel. God is "steadfast love."

Sometimes God appears to abandon us. In reality, we are abandoning him and he is letting us have our way. But this is only temporary. He promises, "With great tenderness I will take you back."

When we sin we are not living up to what God created us to be. Or to the divine life he gave us. But we are also preventing God from being—or showing, at least—what he really is. He tells Israel, "For a moment I hid my face from you," because for their own good he had to act harshly with them, which is not what God wants to do. But God's true self prevails: "With *enduring love* I take pity on you."

God will always rescue us if we turn to him. "Though the mountains leave their place and the hills be shaken, my steadfast love shall never leave you, nor my covenant of peace be shaken." He will do it because the "definition" of God is "steadfast love." When things go bad, we need to keep ourselves *aware* of this.[1]

Luke 7:24-30 ends with a terrible statement: the Pharisees and specialists in the Law, by refusing to receive John's baptism, "defeated God's plan in their regard." Humans can keep God from doing for them what he wants to do, and from being for them what he wants to be. This is the awesome reality of freedom. Having created us with free wills, God will respect the human nature he designed.

But if we don't respect his Nature, by that act we "defeat God's plan in our regard." By "destroying" what God should be for us, we destroy ourselves.

Authentic *Fear of the Lord* keeps us aware of this: aware of what God is and of what we are. Of the distance between us. But also of the "grace of our Lord Jesus Christ" which overcomes that distance with divine power and makes us one with God in the intimacy of sharing his own life.

I will praise you, Lord, for you have rescued me.

---

[1] See *John* 1:14. Scripture uses the phrase "steadfast love" 173 times. *Hesed* and *emet* are the key characteristics of God in *Exodus* 34:6. (And see *Psalms* 86:15; 103:8). They are also translated as "grace and truth," kindness and fidelity," and "enduring love" (1970 New American Bible).

Initiative: Live in the "fear" that is absolute confidence in God.

Third Week of Advent — Friday

December 16, 2011

O God, let all the nations praise you!
(Responsorial: Psalm 67)

We don't walk around all day conscious that we are Americans. That is something we just take for granted until something calls our attention to it. Like a war, a national disaster, or on a more ordinary level, paying our taxes. Or when something happens that just makes us proud to be an American. But we should not simply take for granted being children of God, "citizens with the saints and also members of the household of God."[1]

Isaiah 56:1-8 makes the point that covenanted relationship with God is not something we are just "born into." It is open to all: "Let not the foreigner say, when he would join himself to the Lord, 'The Lord will surely exclude me from his people.'" No one is excluded. But we should keep *aware* that we are Christians by a special, personal invitation from God.

For God—and explicitly in the "catholic," "universal" Church—cultural differences simply enrich the People of God. No culture is "better" or "worse" than another in any absolute sense. The only question is, "What language, symbols, and ceremonies will most effectively communicate the faith to these particular people? What customs, practices, laws, and liturgy will help them enter more easily into intimate knowledge and love of Jesus Christ?" There are over twenty different *rites* in the Church, because, "My house shall be called a house of prayer for *all* peoples." We respond, *"O God, let all the nations praise you!"*—each according to the richness and diversity of its own tradition.

John 5:33-36 alerts us to the sad fact that "cultural prejudices" extend to more than national customs. We have our little litmus papers by which we judge whether someone is "liberal" or "conservative." We measure people by the devotions and practices they do or do not embrace. We judge them by whether they are adhering externally to Church laws—for example, whether or not they are married "in the Church." Jesus rejects any judgment that does not look to the heart.

Many believed the testimony of John the Baptizer because his way of life was so austere. But John's true holiness consisted in his gift of sharing in the life of God, not in his works. When we judge others, we need to keep aware that it is the invisible gift of grace that sanctifies, not external performance. And we cannot see into another's heart.

When Jesus says, "The very works which I perform testify on my behalf," he was talking about works only God can do. When we can't find any explanation for why people would act as they do except deep faith in God's words, hope in his promises, and love without human rewards, this is strong evidence of a graced heart. We accept anyone whose life shows signs of grace. *"O God, let all the nations praise you!"*

---

[1] Read *Ephesians*, chapter 2.

Initiative: Be aware that grace in the heart is a mystery. Do not judge.

FOR REFLECTION AND DISCUSSION: THIRD WEEK OF ADVENT

Jesus Saves Us From Sin.

Being "children of the Father" makes us holy.

Invitation: To be *aware* that the Lord is near.

For prayer and discussion: How many of these statements do you feel you understand? How often are you consciously aware of them?

Sunday: To convince others that Jesus is good news we have to experience him as good news in our own lives. And be able to say, "In my God is the joy of my soul."

The good news is that *Jesus* is here, *Jesus* is at work, *Jesus* is saving us, *Jesus* has made and is making us holy.

To be "holy" means to be "set apart" by God, chosen, blessed, sanctified by the gift—the pure gift—of his "sanctifying grace," the *favor of sharing in the life of God*.

Monday: The more we are *aware* of Christ's presence in us, the more we will *evangelize* by showing the face of Christ in our own milieu.

Faith is the *gift of sharing in God's own act of knowing*. We know as Jesus knows, because by Baptism we have *become Christ*. We know the Father as only the Son can know him, because "in Christ" we are the sons and daughters of God.

Tuesday: The triumphalist image is the opposite of the "pilgrim Church" image adopted by the bishops in Vatican II. They admitted that false or careless teaching of Catholic doctrine contributed to the "rise of atheism."

Wednesday: We need our God and Savior to be near, present to us. If not present to our senses, then present in our *awareness* of what we have seen and heard.

Thursday: God is "steadfast love." When things go bad, we need to keep ourselves *aware* of this.

Friday: For God—and explicitly in the "catholic," "universal" Church—cultural differences simply enrich the People of God.

Initiatives:
During Advent form the habit of touching your heart frequently during the day and saying the WIT prayer: "Lord, live with me; live in me; live through me."
Believe and be aware that God is "with you." Let him act in you and through you.
Be aware of what you know by faith and of all who know it with you.
Be aware of the "No" in you at war with the "Yes" you say to God.
Remain aware of what you have "seen and heard." Keep the faith.
Live in the "fear" that is absolute confidence in God.
Be aware that grace in the heart is a mystery. Do not judge.

"O" Antiphons

Explanation adapted from The Roman Catholic Lectionary Website
http://catholic-resources.org/Lectionary/Advent-O-Antiphons.htm
compiled by Felix Just, S.J., Ph.D.

From December 17 to 23, there are special Masses and Lectionary Readings that take precedence over the ordinary weekdays (but not Sundays) of Advent.

For these seven days, during the Evening Prayer of the Liturgy of the Hours (Vespers) the Antiphons that introduce the reciting or singing of Mary's hymn, the *Magnificat* (*Luke* 1:46-55), all begin by addressing Jesus by a special title preceded by the exclamation "O." They are called the *"O" Antiphons.* Each Antiphon calls on the Messiah to come, beginning with a biblical title and closing with a specific petition.

These seven traditional "O" Antiphons are more than a thousand years old. Since the Second Vatican Council, they have been adapted (slightly reworded and rearranged) for the "Alleluia Verse" of the Mass:

O Wisdom of our God Most High, guiding creation with power and love: come to teach us the path of knowledge!

O Leader of the House of Israel, giver of the Law to Moses on Sinai: come to rescue us with your mighty power!

O Root of Jesse's stem, sign of God's love for all his people: come to save us without delay!

O Key of David, opening the gates of God's eternal Kingdom: come and free the prisoners of darkness!

O Radiant Dawn, splendor of eternal light, sun of justice: come and shine on those who dwell in darkness and in the shadow of death!

O King of all nations and keystone of the Church: come and save us, whom you formed from the dust!

O Emmanuel, our King, and Giver of Law: come to save us, Lord our God!

In the reflections that follow, the Antiphons are a more literal translation of the Latin.

In the traditional arrangement, when viewed from Christmas Eve backward, the first letters of the Latin texts (**E**mmanuel, **R**ex, **O**riens, **C**lavis, **R**adix, **A**donai, **S**apientia) spell out the phrase *ero cras* ("I will be here tomorrow").

SATURDAY THE "O" ANTIPHONS

DECEMBER 17, 2011

O Wisdom

*Word proceeding from
the mouth of the Most High,
Who show us all things framed
between their beginning and their end;
Placing all goods in perspective under
the strong, agreeable rule of truth;
Come, teach us the lifegiving way,
Come, show us the path of salvation.*

Both **Genesis 49:2-10** and **Matthew 1:1-17** introduce people as having roles and relationships to respect. The *Responsorial* tells the fruit of respecting the role of the Messiah-King: *"Justice shall flourish in his time and fullness of peace forever."* Jesus *"guides creation with power and love."* As *Wisdom*.

An eight-year-old asked me at Christmas, "Why does God get to live forever and we don't? It's not fair."

Nothing he had seen, either at home or in school, had given him any sense of perspective about God. I thought, "The beginning of *Wisdom* is *Fear of the Lord*." Fear, not as fright, but as *perspective*. "God," for him, was on the same plane as creatures.

And adults were on the same plane as children. His mother told me, in another context, that the reason he interrupted conversations and ignored commands was that "he thinks children and adults are equals." And why not?

The key to the problem is *relationship*, which is the basis for *order*. We have to respect what every thing and every person is in relationship to others and ourselves. Interaction and relationship mutually define each other. And imply difference. Enter *Fear of the Lord*.

Seen in perspective, God is Absolute Difference. He is measured by nothing but is the Measure of all things: of all truth and goodness. He is the criterion. We don't ask "why" God does anything except to learn what God is. What God is, *is* the "why" of everything.

If there is no Absolute, then nothing relative has any significance. "Good" and "bad" are just matters of opinion. Delete God and life has the purpose of a pinball (oldstyle): blindly launched, careening unguided off of whatever it meets, to rack up a meaningless score when it drops into its terminating slot.

But if there is an Absolute (recognized by *Fear of the Lord*), then there is a basis for taking relative values seriously—like goals and meaning in life, obedience to parents and to laws, speaking truth, doing justice, and distinguishing between human and animal life when we kill. Life has something to aim at. Enter *Wisdom*.

Wisdom is the "habit of seeing everything in the light of the ultimate end, the goal of life." This is the key to *order*. And order is the key to peace.

Jesus is *Wisdom* made flesh, come to *show us all things framed between their beginning and their end, placing all goods in perspective*. The gift of perspective, *Fear of the Lord*, is both the source and the summit of *Wisdom*.

Come, teach us the lifegiving way,

Come, show us the path of salvation.

Initiative: See all things in perspective. Cultivate *Fear of the Lord* and *Wisdom*.

Fourth Sunday of Advent **Sunday**

December 18, 2011
Jesus Gives Us Divine Life

Forever I will sing the goodness of the Lord.
(Responsorial: Psalm 89)

Inventory
What do I expect Jesus to do for me? Do I expect Jesus to help me be anything more than just a really good human being so I can get to heaven?

Input

In the *Entrance Antiphon* we ask God to let the *"clouds rain down the Just One, and the earth bring forth a Savior."* Jesus is not only human but divine. He comes from both heaven and earth—to give us the fullness of life, both human and divine. This is the *mystery* of his identity and of our identity as divine children of the Father.

In the *Opening Prayer* we ask God to "fill our hearts with *your* love"—the love revealed" in "the coming of your Son as man." But we cannot fully understand Christ's love for us or return it until God leads our minds "through his suffering and death to the glory of his resurrection." Only then can we really know him and love him as he deserves. The love we ask God for is a divine love that responds to a Person who is divine. With this love we can also love others divinely, as God loves them. Jesus came to enable us to do this: to love "in him" as children of our Father.

The Promise

The *Responsorial Psalm* invites us to: *"sing the goodness of the Lord forever"* (*Psalm* 89) and tells us why: because of God's *kindness* and his *faithfulness*; because of the *covenant* and the *promise* he made to King David to "establish his throne for all generations."

The promise was made in **2 Samuel 7:1-16.** David didn't think it was right that he himself was "living in a house of cedar, while the ark of God dwells in a tent." He wanted to "build a house for God to dwell in." But God made him a promise instead: "The LORD declares to you that the LORD will make *you* a house…. Your house and your kingdom shall be made sure forever before me.... established forever."

The "house" God promised David was not just a building of wood and stone. Although he had no idea of it, the house God was promising was the one Jesus had in mind when he said to his enemies, "Destroy this temple, and in three days I will raise it up."

They answered him, "This temple has been under construction for forty-six years, and will you raise it up in three days?"

> But he was speaking of the temple of his body. After he was raised from the dead, his disciples remembered that he had said this (*John* 2:19-22).

45

SUNDAY FOURTH SUNDAY OF ADVENT

The first "house" God gave David was in fact a house for God. It was the womb of one of his descendants, Mary of Nazareth.[1]

God also gave David a "house" in the sense of a *dynasty*. The "house of David" was "established forever" when Jesus died, rose, and established the Church as his continuing body on earth—the body of the "Son of David"—to "endure forever," until the end of time. We, the Church, are the fulfillment of God's promise to David.

THE SON OF GOD

Luke 1:26-38 proclaims the fulfillment of God's promise to David in explicit terms. To Mary's son God will give "the throne of David his father. He will rule over the house of Jacob [David] forever, and his reign will be without end."

But the key words are, "He will be called Son of the Most High…. The power of the Most High will overshadow you; hence [he] will be called the *Son of God*."

Jesus did not come to be the human savior his People expected. For them the Messiah just meant "the king who would… bring Israel to its destiny…. The title Messiah-Christ meant kingship before it meant anything else; and everything suggests that to most Jews it meant nothing else."[2]

We know, in the light of Christ's death and resurrection, that Jesus was God, the Son of God, who came to make us all sons and daughters of God by sharing his own divine life with us. He did not come just to repair what sin had damaged and restore us to healthy, moral human life. He came to call and empower us to live on the level of God. To understand "salvation" in any other way is to misunderstand totally Jesus as Savior.

MYSTERY MANIFESTED

Romans 16:25-27 proclaims "the gospel which reveals the mystery hidden for ages but now manifested…" Paul identifies this "mystery" as "Christ in you, the hope of glory"; as "Christ himself, in whom are hidden all the treasures of wisdom and knowledge"; as "the mystery of [God's] will…to gather up all things in [Christ]." To know the mystery of Christ as "Son of God" is to know the mystery of salvation: it is to "be Christ" and children of the Father by sharing Christ's own divine life. This is *"the goodness of the Lord"* that *"we will sing forever."*[3]

---

[1]*Matthew* 1:16; *Luke* 1:27.
[2]John McKenzie, *The Power and the Wisdom*, pp. 73, 76.
[3]*Colossians* 1:27; 2:2-3; *Ephesians* 1:9-10.

INSIGHT
What do I understand now as the "fullness of life"? Does "living on the level of God" invite me to change my stance toward anything? Toward anyone?

INITIATIVE
Say the WIT prayer before every action: "Lord, do this with me, do this in me, do this through me." Live as Jesus' body on earth by letting him act through you.

THE "O" ANTIPHONS MONDAY

DECEMBER 19, 2011

O Offspring from the Root of Jesse

raised up as a sign for all people,
Before you the sovereigns fall silent
And hope gathers nations in prayer.
Come free us! Lord, do not delay!

How is it a "sign for all people" that Jesus is an *"Offspring from the Root of Jesse"*? How does this offer a "hope that gathers nations in prayer"?

It is commonplace to think that human beings, nations, and cultures, tend to lose the vision, the ideals, and principles that first brought them together as a people. How many great civilizations flourished and died because the virtues that first kept them together and empowered them grew weak and died out, leaving them corrupt? Where today is the "glory that was Greece and the grandeur that was Rome"? Do Americans today still have the principles, the values, the integrity of our founding fathers?

We can (in fact, we must) ask the same question about the Church. Are we like the early community described in the *Acts of the Apostles*, when:

> All who believed were together and had all things in common; they would sell their possessions and goods and distribute the proceeds to all, as any had need.
>
> Day by day, as they spent much time together in the temple, they broke bread at home and ate their food with glad and generous hearts, praising God and having the goodwill of all the people. And day by day the Lord added to their number those who were being saved.

The answer is "No—but Yes." St. Paul's letters show the early Church had its faults and factions. And the chain of canonized (which means officially recognized) saints through every century shows that the Spirit remains alive and effective in the Church of every place and period in history. But there is a "root" assurance that is more than a play on words.

In calling Jesus *"Offspring from the Root of Jesse"* the liturgy proclaims that in Jesus God himself became a member of this unstable human race. And of one of its yo-yo cultures that kept going up and down through fidelity and infidelity to the law. *"Sovereigns fall silent and hope gathers nations in prayer"* when we see how God preserved Israel, and then his Church, in spite of all sins. Jesus born of human stock, Jesus present among us as one of us, encourages us to pray in every age, *"Come free us! Lord, do not delay!"*

In both **Judges 13:2-25** and **Luke 1:5-25** God brings life out of barrenness. He did it to show two things: that he can work through inadequate human instruments; and that when he does, the results we see are divine. Both Manoah's wife and Elizabeth had children chosen by God.

Every baptized Christian is born of a womb incapable of giving divine life; then reborn "of water and the Spirit." "What is born of the flesh is flesh, and what is born of the Spirit is spirit"— and will live—and last—forever. Stay aware of that and trust.[1]

[1] *John* 3:1-8.

Initiative: Be aware that the life in you is as miraculous as the Virgin Birth.

TUESDAY THE "O" ANTIPHONS

DECEMBER 20, 2011

O Key of David

*and scepter of the house of Israel,
You open wide and no one closes;
You close fast and no one opens.
Come—lead out the bound ones
from their imprisoning retreat
where they sit in darkness
and in the shadow of death.*

There was a magic door that opened into Narnia, land of dreams and divine presence, where Aslan the Lion enabled children to overcome evil.

We have such a door. And we have the key to it. Jesus, as *"Key of David,"* opens to us the door to heaven—the essence of which we enjoy already here on earth by sharing in God's own divine life and joy. Jesus is the key to the fullness of life, here and hereafter.

To many people a "full life" means life that is productive and satisfying by human standards. A ten-ounce glass is full when ten ounces are poured into it. But Christians have become "new wineskins," and the wine we can contain is without dimensions. Life "to the full" for us means life that is "fully human and fully divine."

Because Jesus was God, we believe that all his human actions had divine value. Because he was human, we know now that human actions, human words and gestures, can be the actions of God. He is the fulfillment of the promise in **Isaiah 7:10-14**:

> The Lord himself will give you a sign. Look, the young woman... shall bear a son, and shall name him Emmanuel [which means "God with us"].

To know Jesus as "God with us" and ourselves as "with God" in him, is to know Christ, Christianity, and ourselves.

Baptism transformed us. Made us "new wineskins." The true expression of this mystery is that we have "become Christ"—the words of St. Augustine, included in the *Catechism of the Catholic Church.* If they shock us, it means we have not been shocked as we should have been by the mystery of the Good News. Understanding Jesus as being both human and divine, and understanding ourselves "in Christ" as also being human and divine, is the key to Christianity.[1]

Because we are divine, we believe that our human actions can have divine value. Because we, though human, are the "body of Christ," we believe our human words and actions can be the actions of Jesus himself acting "with us, in us, and through us." This is the key to Christian living.

Does an angel need to tell you, as one told Mary in **Luke 1:26-38**: "Do not fear... You have found favor [grace] with God"? Do you believe that at Baptism "the Holy Spirit [came upon] you," so that the "holy offspring" to be *reborn* would be called son, daughter of God? The key to believing this is Jesus, *Key of David,* who *opens wide and leads out the bound ones from their imprisoning retreat where they sit in darkness*—into the mystery of God.

[1]*Matthew* 9:17; *Catechism* no. 795.

Initiative: Believe you have "become Christ." Let Jesus act in you.

The "O" Antiphons WEDNESDAY

December 21, 2011

O Rising Dawn

*and splendor of eternal light,
Sun of Justice,
Come! Enlighten those who dwell in darkness and the shadow of death!*

Dawn is not a simple experience. It gives joy, inspires deep thoughts, keeps appearing in poetry. What is so rich about it? *Answers*: The light of dawn is:

1. *Relief* from darkness.
2. *Reassurance*: a new day is given.
3. *Promise*: a new day is a new deal.
4. *Variety in unity*: the same sun is different in every dawn.
5. *Stability with change*: The familiarity of the old; the wonder of the new.
6. *The far made near*: The "dawn's early light" comes from the sun, ninety million miles away. But it shines and warms here on earth.
7. *The near made far*: we realize our tiny planet is part of an immense universe. This expands our horizons.
8. *The large made small*: Our earth seems large to us; but a million planet earths would fit inside the sun.
9. *The small made large*: The extent of the Universe dwarfs our imaginations. But none of it is beyond what we can know. Our minds can embrace all reality.
10. *Power made gentle*: On its surface the sun is about 10,000 degrees Fahrenheit. At its center, about 27,000,000 degrees. But when its heat reaches us at dawn, it is gentle, comforting, and life-giving.[1]

When we apply all that to the Infinite God come to earth and present in Jesus, what does "O Rising Dawn" say to us?

Zephania 3:14-18 is preceded (v.8) by "Wait for me, says the LORD, for the day when I arise as a witness."

> On that day it shall be said to Jerusalem: "Do not fear.... The LORD, your God, is in your midst."

"That day" is Jesus come to *enlighten those who dwell in darkness and the shadow of death*; the transcendent, never-failing *splendor of eternal light*, the *Sun of Justice* dawning new and different every day in our world, filtered through the changing circumstances of our time and space; the distant God made near; bringing light from beyond creation to draw us into living on the level of God; expanding our world, our vision, our dreams, and destiny beyond the dimensions of planet earth; condensing the infinite power of God into the gentle, empowering gift of the Holy Spirit.

Those who "watch for the dawn," keeping *awake and aware*, will "sing aloud... rejoice and exult" as Elisabeth did in **Luke 1:39-45**. When she "heard Mary's greeting, the child leaped in her womb, and she was "filled with the Holy Spirit." Our experience will be like hers if we *listen, remember,* and keep ourselves *aware* of the mystery of Jesus constantly revealing himself to us in new ways. But we have to "watch for the dawn." Otherwise, we may not notice.

Cry out with joy in the Lord, you holy ones; sing a new song to him.

[1] www.universetoday.com; imagine.gsfc.nasa.gov; enotes.com.

Initiative: Look for the dawn. In every darkness seek new insight into God's light.

Thursday The "O" Antiphons

December 22, 2011

O King of Nations

and desire of all,
The cornerstone of unity and peace,
Come! Save us your creatures, whom
You fashioned from the dust!

When we address Jesus as "King of Nations," we are giving him a political title. We expect heads of government to take charge of "temporal" affairs, whatever is required for our well-being in this world. Politicians, by definition, are "involved." And so is Jesus. His "headline proclamation" in preaching the Good News was, "The Kingdom of God is at hand."[1]

Our assumptions about politicians are based on an assessment of human talents and power. Theoretically, good human laws and good human behavior could produce a good society. But as long as sin abounds it will not happen. Jesus, however, makes a happiness possible *on this earth* that neither comes from nor depends on human circumstances. Or on human power. He gives *Wisdom, Understanding, Knowledge,* and *Counsel* that do not depend on a good school system. He gives a "family bond" of *Piety* that patriotism can never produce. The gift of *Fear of the Lord* achieves order beyond the power of governments. And *Fortitude* from the Holy Spirit converts heroism in the face of difficulties and dangers from exceptions into the rule. These are divine gifts, and only a divine King can bestow them. We just need to be aware of them and ask for them. *Come! Save us your creatures, whom You fashioned from the dust!*

We call Jesus the *cornerstone of unity and peace:* a unity not of imperialism but of *koinonia,* the divine "fellowship" of "communion in the Holy Spirit." And the peace he gives is something the "world" can neither give nor take away. Knowing this, we will "seek peace, and pursue it" with confidence.[2]

The point is, we need to be *aware* of this, of the difference between what human power or circumstances can do and what God can (and does) do. What we try to do or don't have the courage to try to do, depends on what we are *aware* of when we make our choice. If we deliberately cultivate awareness of the divine life, gifts, and power in us, we will not unreflectively act as if they did not exist. We will use them.

1 Samuel 1:24-28 is the story of a mother who knew the child in her arms was more the result of divine intervention than of human action.

> For this child I prayed; and the Lord has granted me the petition that I made to him.

That awareness determined her action:

> Therefore... he is given to the Lord.

In **Luke 1:46-56** Mary's hymn of praise came out of awareness of what God was doing in her: "My soul magnifies the Lord...for the Mighty One has done great things for me." That should be our constant hymn of praise.

---

[1] For the Jews of his time, "Messiah" meant king, and for most of them it meant nothing else, John McKenzie, *The Power and the Wisdom,* pp. 73, 76.
[2] *John* 14:27; *1 Peter* 3:11a, quoting *Psalm* 34:14.

Initiative: Lift up your heart! Be aware of the divine power given to you.

December 23, 2011

O Emmanuel,

*Our King and our Law,
Long-awaited of the nations,
Savior of all, Come!
Set us free, Lord our God!*

The key to Christianity is *"God be with you."* Or, more accurately, *"God with you."* But we need to understand the mystery of this. And stay aware of it.[1]

The root mystery of Christianity is the union of the divine and human in *God the Son* made flesh in Jesus. We celebrate this at Christmas. Jesus is "Emmanuel," which means "God *with us.*" Even children understand this.

We don't always explain to children the deeper mystery: that by Baptism we were *incorporated into Christ* on the cross. We *died in Christ*, as members of his body, and rose in Christ to live now as his body on earth. We are "in Christ" and Christ is *"in us."* We are true sons and daughters of *God the Father* because, and only because, having "become Christ," we are *in* the Son.[2]

Finally the mystery of the Good News was brought to completion by the sending of the *Holy Spirit* at Pentecost. Through this Gift, Jesus acts now, not only *with* us and *in* us, but *through* us. When we, enlightened and empowered by the Holy Spirit, think with the thoughts of Christ, speak with his words and act as his body on earth, the mystery of Christianity is made manifest to the world: *God with us.* "Emmanuel."

Knowing this does not help much unless we keep ourselves *aware* of it. Only then will it enlighten our attitudes, empower our choices, and anoint all our actions with love. The first phase of growth in grace is *awareness*.

To foster this, *form the habit* of saying the WIT prayer all day long. When you wake, give your body to Christ as you did on the day of Baptism and say, "Lord, live this day *with* me, live this day *in* me, live this day *through* me." WIT. Before everything you do, all day, say, "Lord, do this *with* me, do this *in* me, do this *through* me." WIT.[3]

Malachi 3:1-24 and **Luke 1:(16-17) 57-66** both speak of the "messenger" God will send to "prepare the way before me." The messenger was Elijah, who "returned" in John the Baptizer, to "turn the hearts of fathers to their children, and the hearts of children to their fathers.... to make ready a people prepared for the Lord."[4]

The "messenger" today is us, and the One we announce is present in us. If that is not evident, our message is not credible. Christianity proclaims "God with us," Jesus risen from the dead, living, acting, and speaking in his body on earth, the Church. If we keep *aware* of this, we can proclaim it.

---

[1] "To say, '*The Lord with you*' is to affirm the core of God's Revelation: that God himself has covenanted to take up residence among his people. It is to renew, in hope and thanksgiving, the Covenant made through Moses." Cardinal Jean-Marie Lustiger, *La Messe*, Bayard, 1988.
[2] See *Catechism of the Catholic Church*. no. 795.
[3] Read the classic work of Brother Lawrence, *The Practice of the Presence of God*, Institute of Carmelite Studies, Washington, D.C., 1994.
[4] See *Matthew* 11:14; 17:12.

Initiative: Be conscious of Jesus as *Emmanuel* acting *with, in,* and *through* you.

Saturday   Fourth Week of Advent

December 24, 2011

Forever I will sing the goodness of the Lord.
(Responsorial: Psalm 89)

Both readings and the verses of the Responsorial Psalm are proclaiming *the goodness of the Lord*, with an emphasis on his "steadfast love." In **2 Samuel 7:1-16** God reminds David, "I have been with you wherever you went." And he promises to continue:

> I will make for you a great name.... and I will give you rest from all your enemies.... make you a house.... raise up your offspring after you... and I will establish his kingdom.... forever....I will not take my steadfast love from him.

Psalm 89 echoes this:

> I will sing of your steadfast love, O LORD, forever; with my mouth I will proclaim your faithfulness to all generations.... You said, "I have made a covenant with my chosen one.... My faithfulness and steadfast love shall be with him.... He shall cry to me, 'You are my Father, my God, and the Rock of my salvation!'"

All of this is about *awareness*. It is not enough for God to be good, and for us to know he is good. We have to keep ourselves *aware* that he is good. And aware of just how good he is. This is an essential if we want to live an intentional, growth-oriented spiritual life. It is the first phase of growth into the "perfection of love."

Awareness expresses itself, preserves and perpetuates itself, in *praise*. We should insist on it: *Forever I will sing the goodness of the Lord.*

The Church recognizes in the fourth Preface for weekdays:

> You have no need of our praise, yet our desire to thank you is itself your gift. Our prayer of thanksgiving adds nothing to your greatness, but makes us grow in your grace.

God is always aware of his goodness. For us to be aware of it too is the first step toward union with God in love, the first phase of spiritual growth. *Forever I will sing the goodness of the Lord.*

Zachariah's canticle in **Luke 1:67-79**, known as the *Benedictus*, is so filled with rich memories that it has become the climax of the official morning prayer of the Church.

> Blessed be the Lord... he has visited his people... ransomed them...raised up a mighty savior.... shown the mercy he promised... remembered his holy covenant, the oath he swore... that we, rid of fear and rescued from our enemies, might serve him in holiness and righteousness all our days....

Memories segue into prophecy. Zachary is speaking to and of us all as he says:

> And you, child, will be called the prophet of the Most High...you will go before the Lord to prepare his ways, to give to his people a knowledge of salvation in freedom from their sins.

Do we believe this? Are we aware of it all day? If so, why have we not yet brought the whole world to Christ? How could anyone be indifferent to the Good News unless those who have heard it are? But if we just keep *aware* of it...

> By the tender mercy of our God, the dawn from on high will break upon us, to give light to those who sit in darkness and in the shadow of death, to guide our feet into the way of peace.

We end Advent exclaiming, *"Forever I will sing the goodness of the Lord."*

Initiative: Give God thanks and praise constantly, to keep yourself aware.

FOR REFLECTION AND DISCUSSION: FOURTH WEEK OF ADVENT

Jesus Gives Us Divine Life.

To know the mystery of Christ as "Son of God" is to know the mystery of salvation.

Invitation: To be aware that Jesus, human and divine, is with us.

For prayer and discussion: How many of these statements do you feel you understand? How often are you consciously aware of them?

Sunday: We know, in the light of Christ's death and resurrection, that Jesus is God, the Son of God, who came to make us all sons and daughters of God by sharing his own divine life with us. He did not come just to repair what sin had damaged and restore us to healthy, moral human life. He came to call and empower us to live on the level of God.

Monday: Every baptized Christian is born of a womb incapable of giving divine life; then reborn "of water and the Spirit."

Tuesday: Because Jesus was God, we believe that all his human actions had divine value. Because he was human, we know now that human actions, human words and gestures, can be the actions of God.

Wednesday: Those who "watch for the dawn," keeping *awake and aware*, will "sing aloud... rejoice and exult" as Elisabeth did in **Luke 1:39-45**.

Thursday: If we deliberately cultivate awareness of the divine life, gifts, and power in us, we will not unreflectively act as if they did not exist. We will use them.

Friday: When we, enlightened and empowered by the Holy Spirit, think with the thoughts of Christ, speak with his words, and act as his body on earth, the mystery of Christianity is made manifest to the world: *God with us. "Emmanuel."*

Saturday: God is always aware of his goodness. For us to be aware of it too is the first step toward union with God in love, the first phase of spiritual growth.

Initiatives:
See all things in perspective. Cultivate *Fear of the Lord* and *Wisdom*.
Say the WIT prayer before every action: *"Lord, do this with me, do this in me, do this through me."* Live as Jesus' body on earth by letting him act through you.
Be aware of mystery when you call Jesus *"Lord"* and God *"Father."*
Be aware that the life in you is more miraculous than the Virgin Birth.
Believe you have "become Christ." Let Jesus act in you.
Look for the dawn. In every darkness seek new insight into God's light.
Lift up your heart! Be aware of the divine power given to you.
Be conscious of Jesus as *Emmanuel* acting *with* you, *in* you, and *through* you.
Give God thanks and praise constantly, in order to keep yourself aware.

WE ARE PASSING FROM THE SEASON OF ADVENT TO THE CHRISTMAS SEASON

Advent lasts from the first Sunday of Advent until Christmas.

The Christmas season continues through the *week after Epiphany*. Celebrate until then. Don't take down your Christmas tree until the feast of the *Baptism of the Lord*. Give Christmas its due.

"Ordinary Time" begins with the feast of the *Baptism of the Lord*, which is the Sunday after Epiphany, January 9, 2012.

The spirit of Advent is *waiting, looking,* and *longing*.

The spirit of Christmas is *accepting, seeing,* and *rejoicing*.

This is a time to open your eyes and accept the Good News:

• **The *Introductory Rites*** of the Mass are a recall of *evangelization*. They echo and summarize the *"kerygmatic"*—initial, "heralding"—preaching of the early Church. We need to participate in them in a way that renews and revivifies our experience of hearing the Good News. This means:

• **Listen to the words.** Listen as if you had never heard them before. Listen as the shepherds did to the angel announcing Christ's birth; as the first converts listened to the preaching of the Apostles.

• **See what is proclaimed.** In your imagination go to the stable to "see this event which the Lord has made known to us." Contemplate what the Scripture describes. Read the symbolism of the decorations in the church. Explain them to your children.

• **Give expression to your faith.** When you make the Mass responses and sing the *Gloria*, listen to what you are saying. Mean it. Try to grow into meaning it more.

Let the Christmas Season be for you a new encounter with Jesus Christ.

The Nativity of the Lord (Christmas) Sunday

December 25, 2011
Being Aware of the Good News

"Forever I will sing the goodness of the Lord."
"Today is born our Savior, Christ the Lord."
Sing to the Lord a new song.
A light will shine on us this day; the Lord is born for us.
Break forth into joyous song and sing praises.
"All the ends of the earth have seen the saving power of God."
Sing to the Lord a new song.
(*Psalm* 89; *Luke* 2:11 and *Psalm* 96; *Psalm* 97; *Psalm* 98)

INVENTORY
This year, before Advent (and the advertisements!) began to focus on Christmas, how often did you think of the gift—the mystery—of Christ's Incarnation and birth? When the Christmas season is over, what will remind you of it?

INPUT
Christmas is the only feast of the year celebrated in three Masses; four if you count the vigil Mass. The readings are listed below. But instead of reflecting on each one, we will simply try to absorb Christmas as it is presented in the readings as a whole. Our guide will be the four *Responsorial Psalms*. Every *Responsorial* will invite us to "Sing to the Lord." For his *goodness* (Vigil); for his *birth* (Midnight Mass); for his *light* (Mass at dawn); for his *saving power* (Mass during the day).

THE VIGIL MASS

Isaiah 62:1-5; *Acts* 13:16-25; *Matthew* 1:1-25.

The *Responsorial* (*Psalm* 89) declares: *"Forever I will sing the goodness of the Lord."* Because God has "made a covenant" with his "chosen one." And each one of us shall say of him, "You are my Father, my God, the Rock, my Savior."

Isaiah goes into detail:

> You shall be called by a new name.... You shall be a crown of beauty in the hand of the LORD....You shall no more be termed Forsaken... but you shall be called My Delight Is in Her, and your land Married.... For as a young man marries a young woman, so shall your builder marry you, and as the bridegroom rejoices over the bride, so shall your God rejoice over you.

Is this reason for us to rejoice? The reading from *Acts* reminds us that the "God of Israel once chose our ancestors... and raised up David as their king." Now, "from this man's descendants God has brought forth Jesus, a savior, according to his promise." And the angel tells Joseph in the Gospel: "You are to name him Jesus, because he will save his people from their sins." Is that not reason to respond, *"Forever I will sing the goodness of the Lord!"*

Sunday The Nativity of the Lord (Christmas)

Midnight Mass

Isaiah 9:1-6; Titus 2:11-14; Luke 2:1-14.

> *"Today is born our Savior, Christ the Lord."*

Psalm 96 urges us to "Sing to the Lord a new song" because, Isaiah says, "a child is born to us..."

> He is named Wonderful Counselor, Mighty God, Everlasting Father, Prince of Peace.

In the Gospel the angels "proclaim good news, tidings of great joy to be shared.... in a manger you will find an infant:

> Glory to God in high heaven, peace on earth to those on whom his favor rests.

The "grace of God has appeared, offering salvation to all humanity." So let us "announce his salvation, day after day."

> Let the heavens be glad and the earth rejoice... for he comes to rule the earth.

"Today is born our Savior, Christ the Lord."

Mass at Dawn

Isaiah 62:11-12; Titus 3:4-7; Luke 2:15-20.

> *"A light will shine on us this day; the Lord is born for us."*

"Light dawns... and gladness... Be glad in the Lord... and give thanks!"

"Say to daughter Zion, 'Your savior comes.... You shall be called the holy people, the redeemed of the Lord.'"

Hearing the Good News, the shepherds said to one another, "Let us go over to Bethlehem and see.... They went in haste and... once they *saw*, they understood what had been told them."

They returned "glorifying and praising God for all they had heard and seen."

Paul explains more deeply:

> When the goodness and loving kindness of God our Savior appeared, he saved us... through the baptism of new birth and renewal by the Holy Spirit.

> This Spirit he lavished on us through Jesus Christ our Savior, so that we might be justified by his grace, and become heirs, in hope, of eternal life.

A light will shine on us this day; the Lord is born for us.

Mass During the Day

Isaiah 52:7-10; Hebrews 1:1-6; John 1:1-18.

> *"All the ends of the earth have seen the saving power of God."*

"How beautiful upon the mountains are the feet of him who brings glad tidings, announcing peace... who says to Zion, 'Your God is King!'"

> They see directly, before their eyes, the Lord restoring Zion... For the Lord comforts his people, he redeems....

"O sing to the Lord a new song, for he has done marvelous deeds. His right hand has won victory for him, his holy arm."

Earthly victories are nothing compared to the power inherent in the Incarnation. What has been revealed to us is truth literally beyond all telling:

> God from God, Light from Light, true God from true God, begotten, not made, consubstantial with the Father.

"In times past, God spoke in fragmentary and varied ways to our ancestors through the prophets. In this,

The Nativity of the Lord (Christmas) Sunday

the final age, he has spoken to us through his Son.... the exact representation of the Father's being."

In Jesus "the Word became flesh and made his dwelling among us, and we have seen his glory, the glory as of an only son, coming from the Father, filled with enduring love."

> In him was life, and the life was the light of all people. The light shines in the darkness, and the darkness did not overcome it.

"To all who received him, who believed in his name, he gave power to become children of God, who were born, not of blood or of the will of the flesh or of the will of man, but of God."

This was the ultimate revelation of God's power: "For while the law was a gift through Moses, this enduring love came through Jesus Christ."

In the baby we contemplate in the crib resides all power that is truly power: the power of love.

God is love. "No one has ever seen God. It is God the only Son, ever at the Father's side, who has revealed him."

God is love. And this love we find present, revealed, and available to us in Jesus Christ.

All the ends of the earth have seen the saving power of God.

Insight

How can we, how could anyone, absorb this message? The readings present Jesus, inviting us to "Sing to the Lord" for his <u>goodness</u>; for his <u>birth</u>; for his <u>light</u>; for his <u>saving power</u>. How many "thoughts within thoughts," and "mysteries within mysteries," do these four phrases contain?

Christmas is not once a year; Christmas is all year long. Just as birth is not a one-time act; birth is the beginning of a lifetime. To celebrate the birth of Christ is to make his life our life all year long and until he comes again.

The key to Christmas is an entrance into <u>awareness</u>. Celebrations end; awareness stays and grows—if we cultivate it.

Initiative

Be practical. Make use of the POCKET GUIDE you received with these Reflections. It will help you BE ALL DAY, EVERY DAY, Immersed in Christ.

In Jesus the Word was made flesh. Became visible. Touchable. Speaking to our human ears. Christianity is God perceptible to the senses. God as a participant in human interactions. We need to use our senses to keep us aware of him.

Use your eyes to read his words, your ears to hear him spoken about, your tongue to praise him. "Sing to the Lord." And hear the Spirit singing and speaking from your heart. Reach out your hand and receive Christ in Communion. "Taste and see that the Lord is sweet." Inhale the incense, the fragrance of the flowers.

And use the POCKET GUIDE for ways to "keep the season in the senses." For suggestions on what to read, how to pray, how to keep yourself aware all day of the goodness, the birth, the light, the saving power of God. Stay aware.

MONDAY ST. STEPHEN, THE FIRST MARTYR

DECEMBER 26, 2011

*Into your hands, O Lord,
I entrust my spirit!*
(Responsorial: Psalm 31)

The *Gift of Wisdom* is defined as the grace-empowered habit of seeing everything "in the light of the last end."

Jesus was Wisdom Incarnate. The last words he spoke on this earth were an acceptance of his "last end," which is the end and goal of every human life: "Father, into your hands I commend my spirit."

In **Acts 6:8 to 7:59,** Stephen, the first Christian martyr, echoed the words of Jesus as he died: "Lord Jesus, receive my spirit." This is the model, and the only authentic form, of a truly Christian death. We live to die, and we die to live forever in Christ. In terms of our own well-being, the most important words we will ever speak are. *"Into your hands, O Lord, I entrust my spirit!"* They bring our life back to its beginning and they are the attainment of its end.

To be able to say these words is not something to be taken for granted, however. There was a time in Catholic history when people were afraid that, even after having lived a good life, they would not have the grace of "final perseverance." The argument was that we can live by the rules of religion day-by-day without ever really coming to terms with how firmly we believe. Then, when the "chips are down" and we are called to abandon everything life offers and go *willingly* to God in death, our faith might fail.

Hopefully, that fear is not the terror it once was. But we should have a healthy respect for the difference between the ordinary acts of faith that take us through life and the extraordinary, all-inclusive, final act of faith that brings us through the door of death. *Fear of the Lord* should give us a perspective on this that makes us prepare seriously for that moment. How do we do that?

Stephen's strength came from his vision of the "end" for which we were made:

> Filled with the Holy Spirit, he gazed into heaven and saw the glory of God and Jesus standing at the right hand of God. "Look," he said, "I see the heavens opened and the Son of Man standing at the right hand of God!"

That is the vision we have to keep ourselves *aware of* in life so that it will be crystal clear to us at death. We should be saying constantly, *"Into your hands, O Lord, I entrust my spirit!"*

In **Matthew 10:17-22** Jesus tells us that we are called on to say these words whenever our faith brings us into opposition with the attitudes and values of this world. "Be on your guard with respect to others...." But he promises, "When the hour comes, you will be given what you are to say." If we keep our sights fixed on the end, we will know what to say, both then and in the present. That is *Wisdom.*

Initiative: Be aware of your beginning and your end. See the present as "between."

The Feast of St. John, Apostle and Evangelist — Tuesday

December 27, 2011

Rejoice in the Lord, you just!
(Responsorial: Psalm 97)

1 John 1:1-4 explains why: "Our *fellowship* is with the Father and with his Son, Jesus Christ." In Jesus, the Word of life, "life was made visible… the eternal life that was with the Father was made visible to us." And John, called the "Evangelist"—the "Good-News-er"—proclaims it to all who will listen "so that you too may have *fellowship* with us."

This is what Christianity is all about: *koinonia*—"fellowship," "community," "communion in the Holy Spirit" with God and with one another in the intimate union of one shared life, one shared light, one shared love.

This life was made visible in Jesus Christ. John testifies that it is "what we have heard, what we have seen with our eyes, what we looked upon and touched with our hands." God's divine life was made visible in Jesus. And it is made visible in us.

We should be *aware* of this, and our awareness should make others aware.

John calls us to make this life visible to one another, "so that our joy may be complete."

In **John 20:1-8** John takes us to the theological root of our belief that God's life is present and visible in every Christian: the resurrection of Jesus.

Beginning with Mary Magdalen's complaint after finding Jesus' tomb empty: "They have taken the Lord from the tomb, and we do not know where they put him," John tells how he and Peter ran to the tomb to see. There they saw "the burial cloths," but not the body of Jesus. And John says of himself, "He saw and believed."

What did he believe? He believed Jesus was risen from the dead. Where did he believe he would find him? In his risen body. Where do we find his risen body today? In all the members of the Church who are Christ's body on earth.

Jesus explained before his death that he had to die in order to rise multiplied in all the baptized: "Very truly, I tell you, unless a grain of wheat falls into the earth and dies, it remains just a single grain; but if it dies, it bears much fruit" (*John* 12:24). The "eternal life that was with the Father was made visible to us" in Jesus. And it is made visible to the world in us, who are his risen body on earth. Jesus is "Emmanuel: God-with-us" in his Church. We find him in the "fellowship," in the "communion of the Holy Spirit" we experience with one another.

Awareness is a vital factor in this. What we are aware of shows in our body language. It comes out in our speech, is visible in our actions. If we have really heard the Good News, how can we not be aware of it? And if we are aware of it, how can we fail to make those around us aware?

"Rejoice in the Lord, you just." Show your awareness that Jesus is among us.

Initiative: Let your inner life affect your external environment. By awareness.

WEDNESDAY THE FEAST OF THE HOLY INNOCENTS

DECEMBER 28, 2011

Our soul has been rescued like a bird from the fowler's snare!
(*Responsorial: Psalm* 124)

We need to read **1 John 1:5 to 2:2** with great attention. There is a significant progression in the thought.

First John says, "If we say we have fellowship with him while continuing to walk in darkness, we are liars."

John's focus here is on keeping the faith in its entirety. But "walking" in light also seems to include living by what we believe. Is John saying we are not in union with Christ if we are committing sins?

His next thought is, "if we walk in the light... we have *fellowship with one another*, and the blood of Jesus his Son cleanses us from all sin." So "walking in the light" is not some private adherence to truth; it involves interaction with the *community* of faith. Do we truly have the faith if we do not "assemble" with others for Mass?

Many stop going to Mass because they have been told they cannot receive Communion and so are not in complete "fellowship." ("Communion" and "fellowship" are both translations of the same word: *koinonia*).

John goes on, "If we say, 'We are free of the guilt of sin, we deceive ourselves.'" So committing sins must be compatible with "walking in the light" and being in "fellowship."

The key seems to be in the *recognition* of sin as sin. John continues: "If we *acknowledge* our sins, he who is just... can be trusted to forgive our sins." He adds, significantly, "And cleanse us from every wrong."

Bottom line: "I am writing this to keep you from sin. But if anyone should sin:

> we have an advocate with the Father, Jesus Christ the righteous, and he is the atoning sacrifice for our sins, and... for the sins of the whole world."

It is bad to sin. But it is worse to rationalize and refuse to confess it. And even worse to just "drop out" of the fellowship and stop receiving Communion. Receiving Communion does not say we have no sins. It says we admit them, are trusting in God, and hope one day to say, *"Our soul has been rescued like a bird from the fowler's snare."* Our trust is in Jesus, and in his "atoning sacrifice" to which we are present at Mass.

Receiving Communion does not say we are keeping all the laws. It says we are sinners with hope.

In **Matthew 2:13-18** God appears to be the sinner! Would you want the job of explaining to those mothers in Bethlehem why God let their babies be massacred? Better not to try. Sometimes we just have to believe in God's love for us in spite of apparent contradictions.

And sometimes we have to believe in our love, and others' love for God, in spite of obvious sins. If we can do one, perhaps we can do the other.

We need to keep ourselves *aware* of more than sin.

Initiative: Don't limit your focus to awareness of what you do. Zoom out to God.

Octave of Christmas — Thursday

December 29, 2011

*Let the heavens be glad
and the earth rejoice!*
(*Responsorial: Psalm 96*)

Yesterday John said Christians who say, "We have no sin" are deceiving themselves. Today, in **1 John 2:3-11** he says, "Whoever says, 'I have come to know him,' but does not obey his commandments, is a liar." Is John contradicting himself?

No, John's words here are God's word, and God doesn't contradict himself. But we need to pay attention to nuances. The Greek word translated as "obey" here is τηρεω, whose basic meaning is to "guard, hold, or preserve." This is the root of the word in *Luke* 2:19: "Mary kept (held, treasured) all these words and pondered them in her heart." To "obey" is the fifth meaning given.[1]

John certainly intends we should obey God's laws. But it would be wrong to see here just external behavior. Only those can say, "I have come to *know* him" who know they are "in him" and share his life because they "walk just as he walked." This is not just to live a moral life, but to "keep his *word*," and especially his "new commandment," to "love one another *just as I have loved you*." This is manifestly impossible unless Jesus is loving *with us, in us, and through us* by sharing with us his own divine life. John is writing of the love "that is realized *in him and in you*."

So John says that in anyone who "keeps his word... the love of God has reached perfection." And who can claim that?[2]

But if we understand τηρεω, not as obeying God's word perfectly in action, but as "keeping" it intact in our heart, preserving it in faith, and *desiring* to live it, then it makes sense to say that, as long as we "keep" his word, we are "in the light" and have *koinonia* with Jesus and each other in the shared Life of God—which is both Light and Love.

The opposite of this is to nurture hatred for others in our hearts: for other persons races, religions, nations, political parties, groups in the Church. Whoever does this is "in the darkness, walks in the darkness, and does not know the way to go, because the darkness has brought on blindness."

Luke 2:22-35 identifies enlightenment with recognition of Jesus. Simeon recognized him because he "awaited the consolation of Israel" with faith and desire. We recognize him by keeping ourselves *aware* of all we have "seen and heard." The Light has come into the world. It has "shone in our hearts to give the light of the knowledge of the glory of God in the face of Jesus Christ." If we cultivate *awareness* of the mystery of his light, his love in us by our *identification* with Jesus, then "the thoughts of many hearts will be revealed" in acts of witness and love.[3]

---

[1] This is true both in Bauer's *Greek-English Lexicon of the New Testament* and the French *Concordance de la Bible, Nouveau Testament*, ed. Sr. Jeanne d'Arc, O.P., English translation *Modern Concordance to the New Testament*, Michael Darton, Doubleday, 1976.
[2] *John* 13:34; 15:12.
[3] *2 Corinthians* 4:6.

Initiative: To know you know Jesus, keep yourself *aware* of what you know.

Friday The Holy Family of Jesus, Mary, and Joseph

December 30, 2011
The Family Aware of God

Blessed are those who fear the Lord and walk in his ways.
(Responsorial: Psalm 128)

Inventory

Whether you are married or not, have children or not, what does "posterity" mean to you? Is it important that God should say to you, "Blessed is the fruit of your womb" or "the fruit of your *life*"? What do you want your life to leave behind?

Input

The Feast of the Holy Family focuses on married life. But we should remember that the first, essential, and everlasting marriage in our lives is the marriage every Christian has with Jesus. In Scripture Jesus is called the "bridegroom" and the Church his "bride." Just as there is only one Son of the Father, and the baptized are all "sons and daughters in the Son," so there is only one Bride of Christ—the Church—and all members of the Church are "brides in the Bride." The image used for heaven is the "wedding banquet of the Lamb."[1]

The highest level of mystical experience, and of Christian life as such, is described by St. Teresa of Avila as the "spiritual marriage." To enter into this level of relationship with Jesus Christ is the goal of every Christian spiritual life. It is the "perfection of love."[2]

Our purpose on earth, that makes blessed the "fruit of our life," is to arrive at this level of relationship with Jesus ourselves and to help others to arrive at it. This is the ultimate guiding goal of all relationships (that is, of all *interactions*) within the family and within every other community of faith and love.[3]

That is why, in the *Opening Prayer*, we ask that we might "live as the holy family, united in respect and love"—not just with our blood relatives, but with every member of the human race on earth. We are asking to be deeply united in the "communion of the Holy Spirit," and to experience the love between us as "the love of God" poured out in our hearts, expressed by us to one another.

So we ask that our homes might be previews of heaven, homes in which we experience the "joy and peace of our eternal home" with God. This is the sign that we are living by the Spirit of God: "The fruit of the Spirit is love, joy, peace, patience, kindness, generosity, faithfulness, gentleness, and self-control" (*Galatians* 5:22-23). Where these are the Spirit is, and we are united in Christ. If these are in our home, we will reveal and find Christ in one another.

---

[1] *Matthew* 22:1-14; 25:1; *Mark* 2:19; *John* 2:1-11; 3:29; *Ephesians* 5:21-32; *Revelation* 19:6-9; 21:2-24; 22:17.
[2] See *The Interior Castle*, tr. E. Allison Peers, Introduction, pp. 11, 13, and "Seventh Dwelling Places"; Vatican II, *The Church* no. 40.
[3] A key teaching of Vatican II is that the *laity* are called to perfection and to help bring the whole Church to perfection. "Every Catholic must therefore aim at Christian perfection (cf *James* 1:4; *Romans* 12:1-2) and each... play a part so that the Church... may daily be more purified and renewed..." *Decree on Ecumenism* no. 4.

The Holy Family of Jesus, Mary, and Joseph — Friday

"Blessed Is the Fruit…"

In **Genesis 15:1-6 and 21:1-3** we see Abraham telling God that he counts his blessings as nullified because he is childless: "You have given me no offspring, and so a slave born in my house is to be my heir."

Abraham's culture had little, if any, knowledge of the afterlife. One's value, or at least one's significance for the human race, was continued in one's children. So far as this world is concerned, without posterity one simply ceased to exist.

Even we, who know about eternal life and happiness in heaven, would like our lives on this earth—our "having lived"—to count for something. And God promises us they will. If we believe in his word, his message is, "Blessed is the *fruit of your life*."

For parents the promise is: "Blessed is the fruit of your womb." The children God gives us are destined to live forever, to be our joy forever.

Provided they do not renounce the second birth, birth into eternal life, to which their parents brought them at Baptism. Eternal life depends on their continuing to acknowledge God as their Father by remaining "sons and daughters in the Son," not silencing the voice of the Spirit in their hearts crying, "Abba! Father!" You cannot share the life of your family if you turn your back on your family. And your heritage.

A distressing characteristic of our times is that a shocking percentage of families in our day, in spite of their best efforts, have not been able to pass on the faith to their children. And their children, having renounced their heritage themselves, will not pass it on to the grandchildren. There is no human (repeat: *human*) evidence to tell us that their children or their children's children will "live forever" with the Father, Son, and Spirit, and with all who are united to them in the family of God. Only with insistent faith and "hoping against hope," can we continue to say, "Blessed is the fruit of our womb." But Abraham held to this kind of hope when he thought God was making him sacrifice Isaac, the only son he would ever have. The bottom line is the principle announced by an angel to be the encourgement of every Christian parent: "Nothing is impossible for God."[1]

"My Eyes Have Seen"

In **Luke 2:22-40** Simeon's response when he saw the child Jesus in the Temple tells us how God has blessed us all: "*My eyes have seen* your salvation… a light for *revelation* to the Gentiles and for *glory* to your people Israel."

This is a mystery we have experienced. All those who find Jesus in family life recognize at some point that they have experienced the mystery of *divine enlightenment*. It is important to recognize and to own this. Christian family life is not just human: it is living in the mystery of divine truth, expressed and *experienced* in the home. It is the parents' task to make this happen.

The enlightenment we are talking about is not some ecstatic emotional moment of "mystical illumination." It comes like the dawn, gradually. We are sitting in the early morning darkness, and at some point we realize we are able to see—but we cannot pinpoint the particular moment when that happened. We just know there was a "before" when

Friday   The Holy Family of Jesus, Mary, and Joseph

we could not see, and an "after" when we could. The experience of divine enlightenment is like that.

We have been hearing the truth of God, living the truth of God, and experiencing the fruits of living that truth for years in our family while hardly noticing it. Then one day we realize we "see" God's truth more clearly and *appreciate* it more than those whose family life is not explicitly focused on it. Then we say, like Simeon, "my eyes *have seen* your salvation." I have seen it at home.

Hopefully, we have also experienced this within the "assembly" (congregation) at Mass, and among our believing friends and co-workers, wherever "communion in the Holy Spirit" is made visible.

This is the reward of explicit efforts to live our lives together on the level of *mystery*. Just learning our religion at church or in school will not do it. Nor will just keeping the rules and following the practices of our religious culture: going to Mass, receiving the sacraments, putting up a Christmas crib, getting ashes at Lent. All these help, but they can be more cultural than mystical experiences. Our lifestyle at home, above all, has to help us *experience God*. And that depends, first of all, on the level of *conscious awareness* the parents are able to maintain in themselves and stimulate in their children.

Many ways of doing this are suggested in these *Reflections*. Here we just zoom in on the importance of being *aware* of the deeper truth embodied in words and actions we take for granted: divine truth, revealed truth, truth only accessible through the divine gift of faith.

For example, we see in each other the same human nature, human characteristics, and qualities Jesus had. Jesus smiled, cooked, lent a helping hand, felt compassion, spoke with insight, got tired and, yes, showed impatience (*Matthew* 17:17). When we see these realities in one another we need to remind ourselves they were also visible in Jesus, God-made-flesh; and when they are visible in us, his body on earth, Jesus is visibly acting.

Especially when we recognize the action of *grace* in one another: a word or deed, an attitude, stance, or choice that cannot be explained by human reason or motivation alone. Then we realize we are in living contact with Jesus in the flesh. In our family. Among our friends.

In the *sacraments* we need to make ourselves and our children aware that Jesus himself is present and acting: consecrating us in Baptism as "prophets, priests, and stewards of his kingship," forgiving our sins, giving himself to us in Communion, strengthening us in sickness, saying "yes" over and over again *with us, in us, and through us* in the marriage vows. And especially that at Mass we are present to Jesus offering himself for us in love, asking us to offer ourselves with him and in him as his body, our "flesh for the life of the world."

Obviously, there is no such thing as a Christian family life in a family that does not gather daily to pray together. The prayer has to be so short and so appealing that it is not a turn-off for children. Ideally it should include, at some time during the week, a tiny bit of Scripture reading. With private follow-up encouraged for those who are able. This is not commonplace in our country. Which may partly explain why defections are commonplace.

Looking Forward...

Hebrews 11:8-19 exhorts us to live out our faith by recalling the example of our ancestors, especially Abraham, whom we call in the Mass our "father in faith."

> By faith Abraham obeyed when he was called to set out for a place that he was to receive as an inheritance; and he set out, not knowing where he was going.

Our religion, as experienced in family life, should be a conscious journey into something yet unknown. Into deeper experience of God. Into clearer understanding of the Scriptures. An experience of continual changes in lifestyle as different members get insights into how to embody the values of Jesus more evidently. Of growth into greater appreciation of each other, especially through sharing experiences of faith and prayer. Into more responsible involvement in the work of transforming society, even in miniscule ways at home and at school, in social life, sports, and church.

And, yes, we can and must experience our family life as something different from American culture. Abraham, Isaac, and Jacob, even in the land promised to them, were there "as in a foreign land, living in tents." They "looked forward to the city that has foundations, whose architect and builder is God." Christian parents should impress upon their children that, even while we accept all that is good in our culture and try to improve it, we know that "here we have no lasting city, but we are looking for the city that is to come." While we do our civic duty, work and vote for better government, we are very aware that "our citizenship is in heaven, and it is from there that we are expecting a Savior, the Lord Jesus Christ."[2]

Christians are by definition countercultural. If we just encourage our children to "fit in," we will see them follow the culture right out of the Church. Jesus said to his disciples:

> Because you do not belong to the world, but I have chosen you out of the world—therefore the world hates you.[3]

If we are totally accepted in our society, we may have something to worry about.

Those whom *Hebrews* proposes for imitation "confessed that they were strangers and foreigners on the earth." They made it clear they were "seeking a homeland," that they saw and sought something greater than the benefits offered by their society, or any society. This should be evident in the lifestyle of every Christian family.

We are the "pilgrim Church," on the way to somewhere. We "left" this world, and "all its empty promises" at Baptism. *Hebrews* says that if our ancestors "had been thinking of the land that they had left behind, they would have had opportunity to return." The opportunity to give up the quest for the Promised Land and settle for what this world offers is available to our children. And many do turn back to it—and away from the Church and the pledges they made at Baptism. Families need to nurture in themselves and their children a conscious "desire for a better country, that is, a heavenly one."

Friday The Holy Family of Jesus, Mary, and Joseph

"By faith Abraham... was ready to offer up his only son." It should be clear that Christian parents would rather see their children failures by society's standards than mediocre in their faith. They make this clear through their priorities in spending time, money, and energy.

To live for God's promises is the definition of *Wisdom*. And the "beginning of *Wisdom* is *Fear of the Lord*. This fear is not fright, but *perspective*. It is seeing this world and everything in it in relationship to the all-inclusive goodness of God. God who is All.

If parents are able to build a family life in which all things are kept consciously in perspective, they will nurture eternal life in their children. *Blessed are those who fear the Lord and walk in his ways.*

It has been said that a monastery is a created environment designed to reflect back the faith-vision in the heart. This applies to homes as well. It is not exactly the same vision—a home should *not* look like a monastery. But living in a Christian home should be the experience of life in an environment that through sights and sounds (and the absence of some sights and sounds), through all that is seen, heard, used, eaten, drunk, and enjoyed, keeps everyone joyfully aware of God and of the Good News of Jesus Christ.

That is a project to invite creativity!

> Happy is everyone who fears the LORD, who walks in his ways.
>
> You shall eat the fruit of the labor of your hands; you shall be happy, and it shall go well with you. Your wife will be like a fruitful vine within your house; your children will be like olive shoots around your table.
>
> Thus shall those be blessed who fear the LORD.
>
> The LORD bless you from Zion. May you see the prosperity of Jerusalem all the days of your life. May you see your children's children.
>
> Peace be upon Israel!

[1]*Romans* 4:18; *Luke* 1:18; 18:27; *Hebrews* 6:9-20.
[2]*Hebrews* 13:34; *Philippians* 3:20.
[3]*John* 15:18-21.

Insight
What new ideas has this reflection given me about family life? Did it upset me or inspire me? How does hope *factor into this?*

Initiative
Sit down with your spouse and older children and discuss how you might make your family life foster a deeper, more constant experience of divine life in you all.

Octave of Christmas — Saturday

December 31, 2011

*Let the heavens be glad
and the earth rejoice!*
(Responsorial: Psalm 96)

1 John 2:18-21 is a troubling passage. We can't help thinking of all those who have "left" the Church by giving up attendance at Mass. Have they really left the Church, or are they just "leaving it alone" for awhile?

They may not have renounced the faith in their hearts. But they have "left" the Church. The word "church" (*ecclesia*) means "assembly." When we no longer assemble with those who believe, we have left the assembly. Left the Church.

We hope they will come back. But John raises a troublesome thought. He says:

> They went out from us, but they did not belong to us; for if they had belonged to us, they would have remained with us. But by going out they made it plain that none of them belongs to us.

When people give up on the Church, does it mean they have lost the faith, or that they never had it?

Faith is a gift. It is the gift of sharing in God's own knowing act. It comes with the gift of "grace," which means the favor of sharing in God's own life. Baptism gives this gift. To infants not mature enough to perform the human "work" of choosing to believe, Baptism gives this gift gratuitously. It is not a violation of freedom to give grace gratuitously to those who cannot exercise free choice. But when infants mature, they must ratify the choice their parents made for them. When John says, "You have been anointed by the Holy One, and all of you have knowledge," he is speaking to those who have.

Four popes have called for a "New Evangelization." They are recognizing that the Church is filled with people who have never really "heard" the Good News. Many of them come regularly to Mass. But they are not on fire. They are not giving out sparks that enkindle others. The Good News is not news to them. It is more cultural than experiential. They do what they should (minimally), but without any true awareness of the mystery they are living. Perhaps Jesus was speaking of them also when he said, "Father, forgive them; for they do not know what they are doing."[1]

But all of us may need forgiveness. If we truly know Jesus, why have we not made him known? If we have heard the Good News, why are we not spreading it through family and social life, business and politics?

John 1:1-18 says that in Jesus "was life, and the life was the light of all people. The light shines in the darkness, and the darkness did not overcome it." In Jesus the light shone because in him the Word was *made flesh*. In us the light will shine only if his words are "made flesh" in our actions. But we have to be *aware* of doing it. Can you say:

> There was a person sent from God, whose name was (say your own). I came as a witness to testify to the light, so that all might believe through me.

[1]*Luke* 23:34.

Initiative: Be aware of your mission. You are "sent" to live light. Give it.

FOR REFLECTION AND DISCUSSION: WEEK AFTER CHRISTMAS

Being Aware of the Good News

The Mystery of the Incarnation is our reason to rejoice.

Invitation: To let this Season of Christmas be a new encounter with Jesus.

For prayer and discussion: How many of these statements do you feel you understand? How often are you consciously aware of them?

Sunday: Now it is possible to say, "You are my Father, my God, the Rock, my Savior."

The "grace of God has appeared, offering salvation to all humanity," and we are "glorifying and praising God for all…[we] have heard and seen," for God has come among us. Now, *"All the ends of the earth have seen the saving power of God."*

Monday: Jesus was Wisdom Incarnate. The last words he spoke on this earth were an acceptance of his "last end," which is the end and goal of every human life: "Father, into your hands I commend my spirit."

Tuesday: God's divine life was made visible in Jesus. And it is made visible in us.

Wednesday: Receiving Communion does not say we are keeping all the laws. It says we are sinners with hope.

Thursday: Only those can say, "I have come to *know* him" who know they are "in him" and share his life because they "walk just as he walked." This is not just to live a moral life, but to "keep his *word*," and especially his "new commandment," to "love one another *just as I have loved you."*

Friday: …living in a Christian home should be the experience of life in an environment that through sights and sounds (and the absence of some sights and sounds), through all that is seen, heard, used, eaten, drunk and enjoyed, keeps everyone joyfully aware of God and of the Good News of Jesus Christ.

Saturday: In Jesus the light shone because in him the Word was *made flesh*. In us the light will shine only if his words are "made flesh" in our actions.

Initiatives:
Use your eyes to read his words, your ears to hear him spoken about, your tongue to praise him. And hear the Spirit singing and speaking from your heart. Reach out your hand and receive Christ in Communion.
Be aware of your beginning and your end. See the present as "between."
Let your inner life affect your external environment. By awareness.
Don't limit your focus to awareness of what you do. Zoom out to God.
To know you know Jesus, keep yourself *aware* of what you know.
Sit down with your spouse and older children and discuss how you might make your family life foster a deeper, more constant experience of divine life in you all.
Be aware of your mission. You are "sent" to live light. Give it.

Solemnity of Mary, Mother of God Sunday

January 1, 2012
The Old and the New

May God bless us in his mercy!
(*Responsorial: Psalm* 67)

Inventory

How do you feel about the New Year? Do you connect it with Mary being "Mother of God"? Are you inspired to make any "New Year's resolutions"?

Input

Recognizing a New Year is combining the old and the new. The length of the year is not arbitrary; we didn't decree it. We *figured out* that it takes 365 days for the earth to revolve around the sun. Because the orbit is elliptical, the distance from the sun varies, giving us hot and cold seasons that make what we call a complete year. Because the earth's axis is tipped over about 23.5° from vertical, the seasons vary in different areas of earth, depending on how direct their exposure to the sun is. This state of things is old! It has been going on for about 4.5 billion years. Every time we say, "Happy New Year!" we are acknowledging an objective order in the universe determined, ultimately, by God billions of years ago. We measure time by it.

At the same time, we know nothing remains the same forever, particularly where human beings are making choices that change the conditions on earth for everyone: for better and for worse. So we hope that the changes during this new year will be happy ones. And we act to make them so, praying: *May God bless us in his mercy!*

Looking Forward

Numbers 6:22-27 echoes this prayer: "The Lord let his face shine upon you, and be gracious to you!" We look forward to the New Year with hope. The *Responsorial Psalm* specifies: "So may your way be known upon earth; among all nations, your salvation." Christians are always *aware* that we have a mission to the world. We cannot rest until everyone on earth knows God's way and follows it into the joy of salvation. But this is not cut-and-dried.

We ourselves must be constantly learning God's way, constantly trying to understand and follow it better. We define ourselves as a "pilgrim Church." We know where we are going, but we are constantly correcting our course. If we ever think we "have all the answers" and need do nothing more than "keep the rules," we have succumbed to the virus of Phariseeism. Jesus said, "Everyone who has been trained for the kingdom of heaven... brings out... what is new and what is old." To settle for what we already know is to reject the unfolding truth of God.[1]

Mother of God

Luke 2:16-21 shows Mary responding to something so new we hardly grasp it. She was invited to become

SUNDAY SOLEMNITY OF MARY, MOTHER OF GOD

the "Mother of God." This just doesn't fit into any rational categories. A creature cannot be the mother of the Creator. Or give life to God. To understand this we have to get into another orbit of knowledge. God's own orbit.

In Jesus, God the Son became human. He was conceived in Mary's womb, not through human intercourse, but by the "overshadowing" of the "Most High." Therefore he is called "the Son of the Most High." Jesus is the Son of God, and Mary is the Mother of God.

Creatures begin to exist when God says, "Be!" And we continue to exist only as long as God "holds the note." But when God the Son took flesh from Mary to make it his body, he stopped giving it created existence by his "Be," and made it, and all of Jesus' human nature, exist instead by his own eternal, infinite, divine Act of Being. In Jesus the voice of God is not saying, "Be!" It is saying, "I AM." The human nature of Jesus does not exist because it was created, but because God is within it, saying, "I AM." And yet, that human nature came from a creature. Jesus was conceived, not just "in" Mary, but "of" Mary. The flesh he took was human flesh. That is why he is truly and completely human, while at the same time truly and completely divine. And Mary is the Mother of "Jesus"; that is, of all he is.

This is a "mystery," which means "a truth that invites endless exploration." For Mary, everything about Jesus was this. After his birth, when the shepherds "made known what had been told them about the child," the Gospel tells us "Mary treasured all these words and pondered them in her heart." She was always trying to enter into new understanding, new appreciation of the mystery of her life and God's. And that is what we are called to do. To imitate this in Mary would be a good resolution for the New Year."[2]

LOOKING INWARDS

In **Galatians 4:4-7** the mystery is extended. Mary, by her "Yes," became the Mother of God. We, by our "Yes" at Baptism, become the body of Christ and "in him" children of the Father:

> God sent his Son, born of a woman... so that we might receive adoption as children. And because *you are children*, God has sent the Spirit of his Son into our hearts, crying, "Abba! Father!" So you are no longer a slave but a child, and if a child then also an heir, through God.

It is as shocking to say we are true "sons and daughters of God" as to say Mary was the "Mother of God." They both depend on the same mystery of the divine and human being united: first in Jesus, who was "Son of God" because he existed by God's divine life; then in us, who are "sons and daughters *in the Son*," because we share in that divine life by incorporation into his body.

This is not something we can understand by being taught the right words in catechism. Or just by repeating them at Mass during the *Profession of Faith*. Our being, the life we live, the life with which we begin this New Year, is a mystery. Our own life is a "truth that invites endless exploration." It is the life of God in us, Jesus' own life that he is sharing with us. To understand ourselves, we must "treasure all these words and ponder them in our heart." We need to keep ourselves aware that our life is a *mystery* to enter into.

Solemnity of Mary, Mother of God SUNDAY

The sad truth is, judging from appearances, at least, most Christians are not bent on entering into the mystery, either of their own lives or of God's. We learned on the first day of catechism that God made us "to know him, to love him, and to serve him." We tend to equate "serving" him with just keeping the Commandments, and few spend any time at all getting to "know him" after the obligatory religious instruction required to receive the sacraments. We should find it hard to claim we "love him" even as much as we love our intimate circle of friends. Whom do we think about more often? In whose interests do we sacrifice ourselves more? With whom do we spend more time?

All that we do for and with our friends *could* be something we do for and with Jesus, of course. If only we have that *awareness* of what we are doing that converts it into a mystical experience. This is the value of saying the WIT prayer all day long.[3]

So how about New Year? This would be a time to ask yourself very deeply—and very honestly—"Am I really trying to *grow* in knowledge, love, and service of God? If so, what is my plan?"

Most people have no plan for spiritual growth. That is why for centuries we taught that the vowed life in religious orders is the *only* "way of perfection." They have a "Rule," a specific way of living designed and approved by the Church as an authentic way to grow into deeper union of mind, will, and heart with God. They have a plan. Laity don't. But everyone should.

"To fail to plan is to plan to fail." Be honest: if you have no plan for spiritual growth you have chosen not to be a fully authentic Christian. Your religion is to affirm Catholic doctrine (mysteries that invite "endless exploration," but which you are not exploring); to keep "in bounds" by obeying the rules; and to maintain a certain level of devotion by observing the Catholic "practices" of attending Mass (probably without "full, conscious, active *participation*"); receiving the sacraments in a way that is not a mystical experience; and saying some prayers. If you read Scripture you are an exception. But you need a plan.

Am I being judgmental? Judge yourself.

If God has led you to a plan, examine it. If he is calling you to more, at least consider *Immersed in Christ*. Why would you not?[4]

---

[1] See Vatican II, *The Church*, chapter 7; *Matthew* 13:52.
[2] Cp. *Confessions* of Sr. Augustine, Book 10, "O Beauty ever ancient, ever new...." See also *Luke* 2:51.
[3] *Matthew* 25:40. The WIT prayer is, "Lord, do this *with* me, do this *in* me, do this *through* me."
[4] Get the free "Overview" booklet (1-800-325-2511).

Insight
Does the New Year invite me to revise my way of living? Does God?

Initiative
Give a clear "Yes" or "No" to embracing a plan of spiritual growth.

MONDAY CHRISTMAS WEEKDAY BEFORE EPIPHANY

JANUARY 2, 2012

The Memorial of Saints Basil and Gregory

All the ends of the earth have seen the saving power of God.
(Responsorial: Psalm 98)

How do we know we know God? And do Christians know God in a way different from everyone else? **1 John 2:22-28** tells us that the unique experience of Christianity is knowing God as our *Father*. And we can only know him as Father by sharing in the life of the Son—and therefore in the Son's own act of knowing the Father as Father. We experience this knowledge of the Father and this union with the Son when we pray with *awareness*, "Our Father, who art in heaven...."[1]

John says we "know that we know" by two things, both essential: through the *"anointing"* of the gift of the Holy Spirit poured out in our hearts; and through *fidelity* to what we have "heard from the beginning" in the teaching of the Apostles.

Christianity is by nature an experience of the divine in the human and of the Spirit in the flesh. Jesus is God made human. In his human nature, actions and words, we encounter God. And in the human natures, actions, and words of the members of his body on earth, the Church, we continue to encounter Jesus. To reject Jesus in the flesh is to deny the Spirit. To reject the Church is to reject Jesus in the flesh he has today. To deny the Spirit speaking in the Church is to become deaf to the Spirit speaking in our hearts. We simply cannot separate the divine from the human and continue to be Christians. But...

If what you heard from the beginning does remain in your hearts, then you in turn will remain in the Son and in the Father. He himself made us a promise, and the promise is no less than this: *eternal life.*

John 1:19-28 makes clear the difference between religion as just a human way of worshiping the divine, and as a divine way of being human.

John the Baptizer was a human preaching a human gesture. The "baptism of John" was a washing in water as a symbol of repentance. But he said, "Among you stands one whom you do not know, the one who is coming after me; I am not worthy to untie the thong of his sandal." Matthew and Luke add: "He will baptize you with the Holy Spirit and fire." This is more than a human gesture. It is God giving the gift of the Spirit and of divine life. We need to be *aware* of this mystery when we attend a Baptism or think of our own.[2]

What is true of Baptism is true of all the sacraments. An action of God is taking place, a mystery of the divine acting through the human. Sacraments remind us to look for this same mystery in all that we do. Say the WIT prayer!

[1] See *Matthew* 11:25-27; *Luke* 10:21-24. See also the *Jerome Biblical Commentary*, 1968: "Here 'anointing' is an Old Testament figure for reception of the Spirit of God (*1 Samuel* 16:13; *Isaiah* 61:1).... To deny that Jesus is Christ [divine Savior of humanity] is to reject the divine filiation that is at the very heart of Christianity."
[2] *Luke* 3:16; *Matthew* 3:11.

Initiative: Be aware of the mystery of the divine and human united in you.

CHRISTMAS WEEKDAY BEFORE EPIPHANY TUESDAY

JANUARY 3, 2012

The Commemoration of the Most Holy Name of Jesus

All the ends of the earth have seen the saving power of God
(Responsorial: Psalm 98)

1 John 2:29 to 3:6 tells us that the "world," meaning those not enlightened by faith, "does not recognize us." As what? As "children of God." But John insists, "That is what we are."

Do we recognize this ourselves? Do we really see ourselves, accept ourselves, value ourselves, and rejoice in ourselves as "God's children"? If we do, what difference should it make in our lives?

When faith is truly alive, it fills us with a new and special hope. We live with the expectation and confidence that when Jesus brings us into the vision of God, *"we shall be like him, for we will see him as he is."*

This faith in our own identity, and this hope in what we actually will be, encourages us to strive for "the perfection of love," which Vatican II holds up to us as the goal of every authentic Christian lifestyle:

> Every Catholic must therefore aim at Christian perfection (cf. *James* 1:4; *Romans* 12:1-2) and... do their part so that the Church... may daily be more purified and renewed...
>
> Thus it is evident to everyone that all the faithful of Christ of whatever rank or status are called to the *fullness of the Christian life* and to the *perfection of charity*.[1]

If we keep aware that we have "become Christ," that we are children of the Father "in the Son," and that we will eventually be perfectly "like him," it will encourage us to keep trying! "All who have this hope based on him keep themselves pure, as he is pure."

John 1:29-34 tells us that John the Baptizer himself did not recognize Jesus for what he was until he "saw the Spirit descend [and] rest on him." To really "know Jesus," it is not enough to have grown up with him, or grown up in the faith that declares what he is. We have to be enlightened interiorly by the Holy Spirit to appreciate his mystery as the Savior who can actually save our lives on this earth from all that diminishes them (which may be different from what we think!).

To really know Jesus we have to *interact* with him in human ways that are made divine by the "co-action" in us of the Holy Spirit. We have to pray with our *minds*, reflecting on what Scripture says of him. And with our *wills*, putting our faith into *action*, (which is where we realize what our faith actually is). If we do this, we will *"see the saving power of God."*

---

[1] *Decree on Ecumenism* no. 4; *The Church*, no. 40.

Initiative: If you want to know Jesus, know yourself as God's own daughter or son. *Act as Jesus* in everything you do. Say the WIT prayer.

WEDNESDAY CHRISTMAS WEEKDAY BEFORE EPIPHANY

JANUARY 4, 2012

The Memorial of Saint Elizabeth Ann Seton

All the ends of the earth have seen the saving power of God.
(Responsorial: Psalm 98)

1 John 3:7-10 says "Everyone who commits sin is a child of the devil.... Those born of God do not sin." How should we understand this?

John makes the distinction later (5:16-18) between sin that is "deadly" or "mortal" and "sin that is not deadly." For a sin to be "mortal," what is done must be so evil in itself that it is absolutely incompatible with graced love of God and of other people. Contrary to what was taught to generations of Catholics before Vatican II, very few actions are this evil. And the experience of priests in the confessional indicates that the actions that really are this evil are seldom recognized as such by the people who commit them. Think of slavery, the tortures and executions of the Inquisition, the atrocities of war, the mass exploitation of the poor. These sins do not come up in the Sacrament of Reconciliation because they are rationalized—and perhaps, John's letter makes us suspect—because the love of God does not truly exist in those who commit them. "Those who have been born of God do not sin [in these atrocious ways], because God's seed abides in them; they cannot sin [in ways so incompatible with love], because they have been born of God."

To know if we are in sin, we need to look less at laws and more at love. John gives a simple rule: "Whoever does not love does not know God, for God is love" (4:8). If we look at what love has done and is doing in the Church, we will agree: *"All the ends of the earth have seen the saving power of God."*

John 1:35-42 tells us how we come into the experience of loving God as Christians do, which means "as Christ does." It is by encountering God in Jesus himself.

When the first two future disciples met Jesus he asked them, "What are you looking for?" Their answer, though they did not know it at the time, was the basic response of the human heart: "Where are you staying?" What we all are asking, consciously or not, is, "Where does God dwell? Where can we find him?"

If we find him, we will find love.

Jesus said, "Come and see." If we see Jesus, we see the Father (*John* 8:19; 14:9). But no one can tell us about him; we have to "come and see" for ourselves, *interact* with Jesus consciously in prayer and sacraments, at Mass, at home, at work, at school, all day. Then we will know we *"have seen the saving power of God."*

Initiative: If you want to know Jesus, accept his invitation to "Come and see." *Keep looking* for personal contact with him at home, at work, in prayer, at Mass. Say the WIT prayer.

CHRISTMAS WEEKDAY BEFORE EPIPHANY **THURSDAY**

JANUARY 5, 2012

The Memorial of Saint John Neumann

Let all the earth cry out to God with joy.
(Responsorial: Psalm 100)

1 John 3:11-21 asks how we can know we are "committed to the truth" and are "at peace" with God. And the answer is, "because we love one another." We can keep every law made by God or humans, but if we are not loving in our way of dealing with every person we encounter, we are what Jesus called "whitewashed tombs" (*Matthew* 23:27; *Acts* 23:3). We may speak—or even preach—brilliantly about God and religion, but if we are not loving in the way we treat people, we are like "a noisy gong or a clanging cymbal." We may live an impressive lifestyle, either "high" or "low"—being identified with all the "right kind" of people or claiming "solidarity" with the poor—intently bearing prophetic witness to selected Christian values, even heroically putting our lives on the line. But if the spirit of love is not visible in our dealings with every kind of person, we "are nothing" and we "gain nothing" (*1 Corinthians* 13:1-3). The only sure touchstone is love.

But we must love "in action and in truth, and not merely talk about it." John asks, "How can God's love abide in anyone who has enough of this world's goods, but presents a closed heart to a brother or sister in need?" When the cry of the poor is heard and answered, then *"all the earth* [will] *cry out to God with joy."*

John 1:43-51 shows us Jesus winning faith from Nathanael by letting Nathanael understand that Jesus knew his inmost soul. Jesus characterized him as "a true Israelite in whom there is no deceit!" When Nathanael asked how he knew him, Jesus said, "I saw you under the fig tree." He may have been referring to something Nathanael was thinking about under the fig tree (a symbol of messianic peace in *Micah* 4:4; *Zechariah* 3:10); or perhaps he just meant he had seen Nathanael and read his character. In either case, Nathanael knew Jesus was someone who knew the truth about him and accepted him. This is something we all need to realize about Jesus and ourselves. It leads to love.

Jesus told Nathanael he would see "greater things" yet. Jesus, by identifying himself with "Jacob's ladder" (*Genesis* 28:12), was calling himself the bridge between heaven and earth. To know Jesus is to know God. As *Emmanuel*—"God with us"—Jesus makes God humanly accessible. In Jesus we can deal with God as we deal with other human beings. But we need to keep ourselves *aware* of this and constantly *interact* with him. This is a core of Christianity. It is why at Christmas we sing, *"Let all the earth cry out to God with joy."*

Initiative: *If you want to know Jesus, treat him as human. Do everything for him you do for your human friends.* Count the ways and adapt them.

Friday Christmas Weekday Before Epiphany

January 6, 2012

Praise the Lord, Jerusalem
(Responsorial: Psalm 147)

1 John 5:5-13 was written for a very specific purpose: "to make you *realize* that you possess eternal life—you who believe in the name of the Son of God." If we really do *realize* this, what can depress us? No matter how bad things get, the truth is that we have within us the divine life of God. We have the life God has. We need to keep ourselves *aware* of this.

"Eternal life" is not simply the gift of human life extended. "Grace" means the "favor" of *sharing in the divine life of God*. "Eternal" means "that which is without beginning and without end." Only God is eternal. To have "eternal life" is to share in the life of God that is without beginning or end, and without boundaries. It is the fullness of knowledge, love, and enjoyment which we find in communion (shared union) with God and every other person in grace.

We receive this life by being incorporated into Jesus Christ. "This life is in his Son. Whoever possesses the Son possesses life." This is what we proclaim at the beginning of Mass: "*The grace of our Lord Jesus Christ* be with you." No matter how bad everything else is in our lives, this gives us reason to say always, "*Praise the Lord, Jerusalem.*"

Mark 1:7-11 tells us that Jesus baptizes us "in the Holy Spirit." What does that mean?

The gift of the Holy Spirit is the fruit of Christ's death (*John* 16:7) and his "first gift" to his disciples after his Resurrection (*John* 20:22). It is the promised fruit of Baptism (*Acts* 2:38) that frees us from slavery to sin and fear (*Romans* 8:15) and helps us "set our minds on the things of the Spirit" (*Romans* 8:5; *Ephesians* 3:16). The Spirit "teaches" us and "reminds" us of all Jesus said (*John* 14:26), guides us (*Galatians* 5:25) and strengthens us (*Ephesians* 3:16). The Spirit, crying in our hearts "Abba! Father!" lets us know that God is our Father (*Romans* 8:15-16; *Galatians* 4:6), that Jesus is Lord (*1 Corinthians* 12:3), and that our bodies are temples of the divine (*1 Corinthians* 3:16; 6:19). The Spirit keeps us one with each other (*Colossians* 12:13; *Ephesians* 4:3) and gives us "the fruit of the Spirit: love, joy, peace, patience, kindness, generosity, faithfulness, gentleness, and self-control (*Galatians* 5:22). By the Spirit we long for the coming of Jesus and the fulfillment of life in heaven (*Revelation* 22:17); and we experience, "the spirit of glory, which is the Spirit of God... resting on you" (*1 Peter* 4:14). That is why, even in suffering we continue to sing, "*Praise the Lord, Jerusalem!*" We just need to keep ourselves *aware* of the mystery we know.

Initiative: If you want to know Jesus, be aware of the Spirit in your heart. Acknowledge what your heart knows and desires. Follow inspirations of faith.

CHRISTMAS WEEKDAY BEFORE EPIPHANY SATURDAY

JANUARY 7, 2012

The Lord takes delight in his people.
(Responsorial: Psalm 149)

The theme of **1 John 5:14-21** is, "We have this *confidence* in God: that he hears us whenever we ask for anything according to his will."

We know it is "according to God's will" that "life be given to the sinner." This we can pray for with total trust.

> Anyone who sees a brother or sister sinning, if the sin is not deadly, should petition God, and thus [more] life will be given to the sinner.

But John qualifies this;

> This is only for those whose sin is not deadly. There is such a thing as deadly sin. I do not say that one should pray about that.

How should we understand this?

Many sins we were taught to call "mortal" are not. For a sin to be "mortal" there has to be "serious matter." The Church cannot legislate this by decree; the action itself has to be *evil*, not just something that is bad or forbidden. And the sinner has to have "sufficient knowledge" and give "full consent" of will. How often do we see that or experience it in ourselves?

John says we should pray with confidence for those who seem to be stuck in sins that may be quite serious, but not enough to be "deadly." And they should keep praying, confessing their sins as sins and receiving Communion, even when there seems no hope, trusting that God will eventually deliver them.

> No one begotten of God commits sin; rather, God protects those begotten by him.... No one who abides in him sins....God's seed abides in them; they cannot sin, because they have been born of God (additions from 3:6, 9).

In Christians who have not renounced Christ by "deadly" sin God still "abides." Though they sin, they will not succumb to "deadly" sin. They have in them "God's seed" working to deliver and purify them. We do not cast them out of the Church or deny them Communion. We pray with trust for their healing. They are alive.

Those who have embraced *evil*, whose sin is "deadly," can indeed repent. We do pray for them. But not with the confidence that comes from knowing God's life and "seed" is working within them. They cannot be "healed." They need to be brought back from the dead.

"Mortal" sin is not a recurring event, any more than mortal illness is. We don't keep dying and coming back to life. People in real mortal sin have lost the life of God. And because they are dead, they don't miss it! They don't have enough love for God to notice or regret his absence. They are too blind to even know they are in the dark. Anyone able to worry about being dead is alive.

In **John 2:1-12** Jesus "revealed his glory!" by showing us how "the grace of our Lord Jesus Christ" transforms life on this earth. When his disciples saw what 135 gallons of good wine did to that little country wedding feast where there could not have been more than a hundred people, the Gospel says, "They believed in him!" So should we.

Initiative: Look for signs of life in yourself and others. Where life is, hope is.

FOR REFLECTION AND DISCUSSION: WEEK BEFORE EPIPHANY

The Old and the New: The mystery of our being is now intimately bound up with the mystery of the Incarnation.

Invitation: To begin this New Year by adopting a plan of spiritual growth that guarantees mystical experiences in the most ordinary of circumstances.

For prayer and discussion: How many of these statements do you feel you understand? How often are you consciously aware of them?

Sunday: Every time we say, "Happy New Year!" we are acknowledging an objective order in the universe determined, ultimately, by God billions of years ago.

To settle for what we already know is to reject the unfolding truth of God.

It is as shocking to say we are true "sons and daughters of God" as to say Mary was the "Mother of God." They both depend on the same mystery of the divine and human being united: first in Jesus, who was "Son of God" because he existed by God's divine life; then in us, who are "sons and daughters *in the Son*," because we share in that divine life by incorporation into his body.

Monday: What is true of Baptism is true of all the sacraments. An action of God is taking place, a mystery of the divine acting through the human.

Tuesday: To really know Jesus we have to *interact* with him in human ways that are made divine by the "co-action" in us of the Holy Spirit. We have to pray with our *minds*, reflecting on what Scripture says of him. And with our *wills*, putting our faith into *action*, (which is where we realize what our faith actually is).

Wednesday: For a sin to be "mortal," what is done must be so evil in itself that it is absolutely incompatible with graced love of God and of other people.

Thursday: The only sure touchstone of grace is love.

Friday: To have "eternal life" is to share in the life of God that is without beginning or end, and without boundaries.

Saturday: Anyone able to worry about being dead is alive.

Initiatives:
Give a clear *"Yes"* or *"No"* to embracing a plan of spiritual growth.
Be aware of the mystery of the divine and human united in you.
If you want to know Jesus, know yourself as God's own daughter or son. *Act as Jesus* in everything you do. Say the WIT prayer.
If you want to know Jesus, accept his invitation to "Come and see." *Keep looking* for personal contact with him at home, at work, in prayer, at Mass.
If you want to know Jesus, treat him as human. *Do everything for him you do for your human friends.* Count the ways and adapt them.
If you want to know Jesus, be aware of the Spirit in your heart. *Acknowledge what your heart knows and desires.* Follow inspirations of faith.
Look for signs of life in yourself and others. Where life is, hope is.

The Solemnity of the Epiphany of the Lord Sunday

January 8, 2012
Awareness of the Light

Lord, every nation on earth will adore you.
(Responsorial: Psalm 72)

Inventory

What experience have you had of darkness? Did you recognize it as darkness at the time? Have you ever been in a place where no one showed any awareness of God? How did you feel?

Input

What is more common than the light of day? We live and work by it, taking sunlight for granted. But the truth is, sunlight does not belong to our world. The light we have most need of to live on this earth does not come from this earth. It comes from the sun, ninety million miles outside of our orbit. Without light from "outer space" there would simply be no daylight. Or moonlight. Or starlight. We would live mostly in the dark.

Did God guide the Magi by a star to make the point that no one comes to Christ except by following a light that is not of this world?

Not even of this universe. Nor any created light. But light from God alone.

We are a chosen race, a royal priesthood, a holy nation, God's own people, in order that we may proclaim the mighty acts of him who called us out of darkness into his marvelous light.[1]

We need to keep ourselves *aware* of this. Only then will the light within us shine out to give light to the world. Then *Lord, every nation on earth will adore you.*

In the *Alternate Opening Prayer* we ask God to "draw us beyond the limits which this world imposes, to the life where your Spirit makes all life complete." With the light of this created universe we can only *act* within "the limits which this world imposes." To arrive at "the life where Christ's Spirit makes all life complete," we need to keep repeating, "Star of wonder, star of might, Star with royal beauty bright, Westward leading, still proceeding, Guide us to thy perfect light."

[1] *1 Peter* 2:9.

Facts and Promise

Isaiah 60:1-6 is an invitation based on a proclamation: "Rise up in splendor! Arise, shine! For your light has come, and the glory of the Lord shines upon you!"

Without the proclamation, the invitation would have no power. Its impelling force is based on two facts and a promise.

The *first fact* should be obvious, although its reality is misunderstood by

SUNDAY THE SOLEMNITY OF THE EPIPHANY OF THE LORD

many: "See, darkness covers the earth, and thick clouds cover the peoples." Everyone grants there is darkness and clouded vision on earth, but many assume the darkness is just poor judgment, and that the clouds obscure only what unbiased minds should be able to see. And they are right—within "the limits which this world imposes." What they don't see is that every human culture, while better or worse, if not corrected and supplemented by a light that is not of this world, is "darkness."

The "thick clouds that cover the peoples" are the assumptions, common in the defectively educated, that religion is irrelevant and revelation non-existent. They ignore the invitation because the *second fact*—"your light has come"—is not evident to them. The truth is, "Upon you the Lord shines, and over you appears his glory." But they are blind to it. Like those blinded by the lights of the city, they cannot see the stars.

The *promise* is addressed to believers: "Nations shall walk by your light.... Your sons shall come from far away, and your daughters...." Family members who have turned away from the Church will return. Even cultures will be converted and nations walk in justice and peace.

If what? If we "Rise up in splendor and shine!" The light that is within us must shine out. It wasn't given to be covered by a basket. We are meant and sent to be stars: to guide the world to Christ by a light given to us that is not of this world. But we have to be *aware* of it.

THE EPIPHANY

Matthew 2:1-12 tells us the story of the Magi. Presumably, they were "pagan" stargazers who sought to know God by studying the rhythm of the universe. In the stars, whose fire was considered a "pure element," they looked for the God of pure Truth, pure Goodness, pure Being and Life.

So God invited them through a star, a symbol from their own religion. But after they had seen what he called them to see, they "went back to their own country by another route." They were changed men, walking a different path.

And the light was shining within them. They had become stars. They were sent home to let the new light that was in them shine out as a revelation of God. They—they themselves—were now the Light of the world. Isaiah had said to believers, "Nations shall walk by *your* light...." Jesus said to his disciples, "*You* are the light of the world."[1]

In Jesus, "the true light, which enlightens everyone," came into the world. "He was in the world, and the world came into being through him; yet the world did not know him."

> In him was life, and the life was the light of all people... [Yet] his own people did not accept him. But to all who received him, who believed in his name, he gave power to become children of God.

Children of the Father, sons and daughters "in the Son." And, because we are "in him" and he in us, we are the Light of the world.

If only, and only if, we let our light shine.

> The Word became flesh and lived among us, and we have seen his

The Solemnity of the Epiphany of the Lord SUNDAY

glory, the glory as of a father's only son....

Now, however, it is we, the believers, who are the "only sons and daughters of the Father" on earth. Unless his glory is "made flesh" in us it will not be seen in our world. In us "the light shines in the darkness." In Jesus, "the darkness did not overcome it." If in our time, in our country and culture, professional environment, family, and social life, "darkness covers the earth, and thick clouds cover the peoples," it means we are failing to shine.[2]

But if we "let our light shine before others, so that they may see our good works and give glory to our Father in heaven," the promise will be fulfilled: *Lord, every nation on earth will adore you.*

EVANGELIZATION

In **Ephesians 3:2-6** it is evident that Paul was *aware* of who he was, of his call and his mission, and of God's empowering grace:

> I, Paul, am a prisoner for Christ Jesus for the sake of you Gentiles....[because] of the ministry God gave me... the mystery... made known to me by revelation...that in Christ Jesus the Gentiles have become fellow heirs, members of the same body, and sharers in the promise *through the preaching of the gospel.*

The last words say it: everything comes about and depends on "the preaching of the Gospel." Before it can be seen, the light has to shine. "Preaching" the Good News means letting the glory of God's light in us shine out in all we are, say, and do. It is *we* who are the Epiphany. We are the "manifestation of his glory" now, even while we still "wait for the blessed hope and the manifestation of the glory of our great God and Savior, Jesus Christ." We, letting the light of God shine out in us, are the fact that makes the promise credible. We are the "preview of the Parousia." If people don't see the preview, it is not likely they will put much stock in the movie.[3]

The first thing we have to do, however, is cultivate *awareness.* How can we make the life of God in us visible if we are not aware we have it? How can we let the truth we know by God's light appear in our words and actions if we are not conscious of what it is, not aware of what we know? How can we show the "fruit of the Spirit" in our comportment—love, joy, peace, patient endurance, kindness, generosity, fidelity, gentleness, and self-control—if we are not aware of how much we ourselves are loved, what reason we have for joy, how Jesus has given us peace? The first phase of evangelization is *awareness.*[4]

[1] *Matthew* 5:14-16.
[2] Read *John* 1:1-18.
[3] *Titus* 2:13.
[4] *Galatians* 5:22.

INSIGHT
Do I appreciate more how important it is to be aware of the light and life in me?

INITIATIVE
Form the habit of deliberately trying to express divine truth, life, love.

MONDAY FEAST OF THE BAPTISM OF THE LORD

JANUARY 9, 2012
Baptized into Divine Life

The Lord will bless his people with peace.
(Responsorial: Psalm 29)

INVENTORY

How often do you think about the fact that your existence is an ongoing gift? The truth is, we remain in existence only because God, at this moment, is continuing to say, "Be!" How often do you go beyond this and marvel that, in addition to what you feel and experience as human life, God is also giving you divine life? He is sharing with you the Life by which he, God, has existed from all eternity and will exist for all eternity. You are living now with *eternal life*. How much of the time are you aware of this?

INPUT

The *Entrance Antiphon* shows God the Father evangelizing by introducing Jesus to the world: "This is my Son, the Beloved, with whom I am well pleased." Doesn't it make us want to ask, "Why?"

The *Opening Prayer* begins to tell us why. We pray that God our Father will "keep us, your children born of water and the Spirit, faithful to our calling." The Father was pleased with Jesus because of what Jesus was: his "Son, the Beloved." And because of what he was going to do: Jesus would make it possible for us to be "born of water and the Spirit." To be also God's children. And the Father is pleased with us for the same two reasons he is pleased with Jesus: because of what we *are*, beloved "sons and daughters in the Son" and because of what we are called to do. In us, Jesus continues his mission, if we are "faithful to our calling."[1]

In the *Prayer after Communion* we ask the Father that "by *listening* to your Son with faith" we might "become your children in name and in fact"—that is, in action. For this we need to keep ourselves *aware* of what Baptism made us.

[1] The 1985 English *Roman Missal* is more faithful to the spirit than to the letter of the Latin by using words that make us more aware of the practical meaning and mystery that inspired the prayer. In Latin "faithful to our calling" is just "persevering in what pleases you." And the alternate prayer, "May we who share his humanity come to share [more in] his divinity," gives theological depth to the anticlimactic Latin "May we who see him as like ourselves externally deserve to be interiorly reformed." The translators were clearly theologians!

THE GOOD NEWS

We cannot read **Isaiah 55:1-11** without being impelled to ask ourselves if we have really heard the Good News. And if we have heard it, understood it. And if we have understood it, kept ourselves *aware* of it. Isaiah cries out, "Everyone who thirsts, come to the waters!" Are we rushing to church, or to any place where we can hear the Good News explained and developed, the way people coming out of the desert rush to a water fountain? When we get off work, do we pick up the Bible before we turn on the television? Isaiah asks:

Why do you spend your money... and your labor for that which does not satisfy? Listen carefully to me, and eat what is good.... come to me; listen, so that you may live....

Seek the LORD while he may be found, call upon him while he is near.

If we brush off Isaiah, will we also brush off God saying of Jesus, "This is my Beloved Son! Listen to him!"?

What we hear from Jesus is not like anything we hear on this earth. God says it through Isaiah:

My thoughts are not your thoughts, nor are your ways my ways, says the LORD. For as the heavens are higher than the earth, so are my ways higher than your ways and my thoughts than your thoughts.

God is offering to let us think with the thoughts of God and live a lifestyle on the level of God. Can we turn that down? Or have we never really heard and thought about what he is saying?

God invites with a promise. If we read his word, it *will* make a difference in our lives:

For as the rain and the snow come down from heaven, and do not return there until they have watered the earth, making it bring forth and sprout... so shall my word be that goes out from my mouth; it shall not return to me empty, but it shall accomplish that which I purpose... for which I sent it.

How can we fail to try something that God himself promises will help us? Are we crazy? Or have we just never really heard the invitation? Never listened.

If we haven't listened before, it is time to listen now. "Seek the Lord while he may be found." And while he is still able to help us be "faithful to our calling." If we are faithful, "*The Lord will bless his people with peace.*"

THE BELOVED

If Jesus teaches us to pray "hallowed be thy name"—to make it our first desire and effort in life that the Father should be known, appreciated and loved—we can take for granted that the Father inspires us to do the same for the Son. We look to the Gospel to find out what we can say.

In **Mark** 1:7-11 we find, first John the Baptizer, then the Father and the Spirit, saying of Jesus, "Hallowed be his name!" To John's testimony the Father adds his voice and the Spirit his confirmation by descending on Jesus in the form of a dove.

"The spirit coming down" is an allusion to *Isaiah* 63:11, 14, where God's spirit is said to have come down upon the Israelites during the Exodus, just as in *Exodus* 19:11, 18, 20, God had come down upon Sinai to form his people. "Like a dove": This was a symbol of Israel in the Bible (*Hosea* 11:11; *Psalms* 68:13; 74:19... *Song of Songs*, 1:15; 2:14; 4:1; 5:2, 12; 6:9) [and] in rabbinical commentaries.... Jesus is thus designated as the representative of God's new people according to the Spirit.... It has ecclesial significance: Jesus embodies the new people of God being born in a new exodus.[1]

In all three Synoptic Gospels (*Matthew, Mark, Luke,* called "synoptic" because they are written from a similar point of view with a similar structure), God calls Jesus "my Son, the Beloved" (or in *Luke* 9:3, "my Chosen") both at his baptism and at the transfiguration. He applies to Jesus what is prophesied in *Isaiah* 42:1-8: Jesus is the unique Son of God, the Servant anointed (as in "Messiah") with God's Spirit.

MONDAY Feast of the Baptism of the Lord

All this will be for us nothing but abstract biblical scholarship—*Wissenschaft*—unless we read the passage from *Isaiah* and meditate about what it means for us personally.

John the Baptizer leads us into it: "I have baptized you with water; but he will baptize you with the Holy Spirit." That is something to think about. And to remain aware of.

What were you taught about your Baptism? That it "washed away Original Sin" and thus gave you a ticket to heaven? True though this is, it reflects a much later focus on Baptism that distracts us from its true mystery.

> The phrase, original sin, so far as we can discover, was first used in the fourth century. The first who used it was either St. Chrysostom, or Hilary.... Soon after Hilary's time, St. Augustine and other Christian writers brought it into common use.[2]

St. Paul presents Baptism as the *mystery* of *dying in Christ* and rising again as his purified body to let Jesus continue his life and mission in us. Baptism is the gift of divine life that makes us true children of the Father "in" the Son. We are "heirs of heaven" because it has become our natural home, not just because our sins are taken away. It is not the absence of sin that gives us entrance into heaven but the presence of God's divine life in us. We may have learned this in the Catechism, but it is probably not what our Catholic culture has made us most aware of.[3]

The essence of our redemption is that by Baptism we have "become Christ." We say to the Father at Mass: "You sent your Son as one like ourselves... that you might see and love in us what you see and love in Christ." The Father now says about each one of us what he said about Jesus: "This is my Son, my Daughter, the Beloved."[4]

THE VICTORY

1John 5:1-9 assures us:

> Everyone who believes that Jesus is the Christ has been born of God.... Whatever is born of God conquers the world. And this is the victory... our faith.

Just to believe in Jesus is already a victory over the darkness of this world and the blind spots in its cultures. But to keep the faith in a way that gives life, we have to remain *aware* of the mystery of graced existence. Then *"The Lord will bless his people with peace."*

---

[1] *Jerome Biblical Commentary*, 1068.
[2] See *The doctrine of original sin... in answer to Dr. Taylor,* by John Wesley, Soule & Mason, 1817, Harvard University, digitized 2008.
[3] *Romans* 6:3-11. See *Catechism of the Catholic Church,* nos. 683, 1265-1274, 1996-1999.
[4] See *Catechism of the Catholic Church* no. 795; Sunday Preface VII for Ordinary Time.

INSIGHT
What more do you understand about Baptism now? And about who you are?

INITIATIVE
Put glasses of water where they will remind you of your Baptism. Bless yourself.

First Week in Ordinary Time — Tuesday

January 10, 2012

My heart rejoices in the Lord, my Savior!
(*Responsorial: 1 Samuel 2:1-8*)

In **1 Samuel 1:9-20** when Hannah asked the Lord for a child, "she conceived and gave birth to a son, and called him Samuel 'since,' she said, 'I asked the Lord for him.'" (Samuel in Hebrew means "the name of God is..." but also sounds like the word for "ask.")

For Hannah, giving life through childbirth was fulfillment. And she begged God for it with such emotion, "pouring out her soul before the Lord," that Eli the priest, watching her, thought she was drunk.

Do we want fulfillment that much? How much do we really care whether our "names" mean anything, our lives count for anything, on this earth? Are we content to just pass through life like a pinball, without purpose or plan, bouncing haphazardly off of one experience after another, racking up random points until we fall at last into the slot that tallies up our final score? Do we call that living?

Thanks be to God, no one has to live like that. Being "saved" does not just assure us of happiness after death. Jesus came to save our lives *on this earth*. And not only from the darkness that distorts our attitudes and values, and from the "death" of destructive behavior; but also from the sluggishness and stagnation of ordinary meaninglessness and mediocrity. No one who believes in Jesus Christ should ever be bored. Or boring to others.

Why? Because Jesus has both called and empowered every one of us to *give life* to everyone we deal with. And to make our environment life-giving. He himself came so that humans might "have life, and have it to the full." And in all who have "become Christ" by Baptism—brought to completion by the "gift of the Spirit"—he continues to exercise his ministry. *With* us, *in* us, and *through* us.[1]

That is exciting; and reason to say: *"My heart rejoices in the Lord, my Savior!"*

Mark 1:21-28 shows us that no one could be bored around Jesus. When he taught, "they were astounded at his teaching, for he taught them as one having authority, and not as the scribes" who interpreted the Law.

Just at the sight of him, "a man with an unclean spirit, cried out, 'What have you to do with us, Jesus of Nazareth? Have you come to destroy us? I know who you are, the Holy One of God.'"

> They were all amazed, and they kept on asking one another, "What is this? A new teaching—with authority! He commands even the unclean spirits, and they obey him."

An exciting man to be around. And still exciting in all who let him work *with* them, *in* them, and *through* them as his body on earth. Where grace is allowed to work, things happen. *"My heart rejoices in the Lord, my Savior!"*

[1] Cf. the WIT prayer: "Lord, do this *with* me, do this *in* me, do this *through* me."

Response: Say the WIT prayer all day long. Make all you do explicitly divine.

WEDNESDAY First Week in Ordinary Time

January 11, 2012

Here am I, Lord, I come to do your will!
(Responsorial: Psalm 40)

1 Samuel 3:1-20 tells us how Samuel came to recognize the voice of the Lord and to know when God was speaking to him. This is what made him a *prophet*.

The reading begins: "It was rare for the Lord to speak in those days; visions were uncommon." Many think this is true in our time. And we may identify with the description: "Samuel did not yet know the Lord, and the word of the Lord had not yet been revealed to him."

But the truth is, we do "know the Lord." We just may not be *aware* of it. We know him with the divine knowledge that comes with the gift of faith. But we will not be conscious of knowing him until we translate this into human knowledge by reading and reflecting on the human character of Jesus as revealed in the Scriptures. When we *express* our thoughts about him—to ourselves or others—in human words, that is when we realize we know him. But it is really the voice of the Spirit in our hearts.[1]

And the "word of the Lord has been revealed to us." We just hesitate to say we have divine *enlightenment*, even though we know that Jesus calls us the "light of the world." He says that what makes his followers different is that they do not "walk in darkness but have the light of life." It is us he is talking about. But if we do not keep ourselves aware that we have the light of light, we will not be attentive to walking in it. And we will fail to share our light with others as *prophets*.[2]

We don't think of ourselves as prophets, even though at Baptism the Lord himself consecrated all of us *prophets, priests,* and *kings.* We just never think about it.

The reading continues; "Samuel grew up and the Lord was with him.... And all Israel ... came to know that Samuel was accredited as a prophet of the Lord." The Lord is with us too. We proclaim it repeatedly at Mass. *Dominus vobiscum* is not just a wish: "The Lord *be* with you," but also a statement of fact: "The Lord *is* with you." When we grow up sufficiently in the faith to be constantly aware of this, everyone who knows us should recognize that we too are "prophets of the Lord."

They will recognize it if our way of living, speaking, and acting makes it obvious that the enduring refrain of our hearts is: *Here am I, Lord, I come.*

Mark 1:29-39: The morning after an evening spent curing the sick, Jesus "went out to a deserted place, and there he prayed." When his disciples found him, he said, "Let us go on to the neighboring towns, so that I may proclaim the message there also; for that is what I came out to do." Jesus was aware of his identity and his mission.

---

[1] *1 Corinthians* 12:3; *Romans* 8:15-16; 10:9.
[2] *Matthew* 5:14; *John* 8:12.

Response: *Know yourself* as empowered by grace. Live as human and divine.

First Week in Ordinary Time Thursday

January 12, 2012

Save us, Lord, in your mercy.
(Responsorial: Psalm 44)

In **1 Samuel 4:1-11** God punished the priest Eli, and Israel with him, "because his sons were blaspheming God, and he did not restrain them." God had sent word to Eli, "The fate of your two sons… shall be the sign to you—both shall die on the same day. I will raise up for myself a faithful priest, who shall do according to what is in my heart."[1]

When the Philistines attacked, "Israel was defeated, and they fled, everyone to his home… Of Israel thirty thousand foot soldiers fell. The ark of God was captured; the two sons of Eli… died."

In modern terms, what God punished Israel for was "clericalism." Because Eli was the priest, and seen as so sacred he was above other people, his sons were able to steal from the offerings people made, and even abuse women, and no one, including Eli, did anything about it.

Because of the clericalism in today's Church, both the laity and clergy, including bishops, refrained from calling the police when priests abused children. This caused enormous suffering to the victims. And the spiritual "Philistines" were able to use it to attack the Church in particular and religion in general. How many Christians, as a result, have given up the fight and "fled, everyone to his home"?

When we look upon any class or category of Christians as "more sacred" than others, we have ceased to be aware of the true mystery of grace. By Baptism every one of us became a son or daughter of God himself through incorporation into Jesus, the "only Son of the Father." Because we are "in Christ," we share in his own divine life. We are divine. Every one of us. And no sacrament, position, or title in the Church makes anyone "more divine" than another. The mystery of our being is that we have "become Christ." There simply is no dignity "higher" than that. "There are varieties of gifts, but the same Spirit," varieties of functions in the Church, but only one body of Christ, in which all are equally members. It is essential that we keep ourselves *aware* of this. Then, no matter what happens, we will be able to say with confidence, *"Save us, Lord, in your mercy."*[2]

Mark 1:40-45 shows us two things about Jesus: First, he is able to heal and cleanse us—and the whole Church—of anything. He said to a leper, "Be made clean!" And, "Immediately the leprosy left him, and he was made clean."

Second, he acknowledged, respected, and made use of the official role of the priests in his day. He told the healed leper, "Go, show yourself to the priest, and offer for your cleansing what Moses commanded." The positions and functions in the "institutional Church" were established by God himself. We don't have to believe the ministers are holier than others in order to use them.

---

[1] See 2:34-5; 3:13.
[2] See *Catechism of the Catholic Church*, no. 795; *1 Corinthians*, chapter 12.

Response: Remind yourself, when you show respect to anyone, that all are equal.

FRIDAY FIRST WEEK IN ORDINARY TIME

JANUARY 13, 2012

Forever I will sing the goodness of the Lord.
(*Responsorial: Psalm* 89)

Too few people are aware that the bishops at Vatican II called on every Catholic to "undertake with vigor the task of renewal and reform" in response to abuses in the Church:

> For although the Catholic Church has been endowed with all divinely revealed truth and with all means of grace, her members fail to live by them with all the fervor they should. As a result, the radiance of the Church's face shines less brightly... and the growth of Christ's kingdom is retarded.
>
> Every Catholic must therefore aim at Christian perfection and... all play their part so that the Church, which bears in her own body the humility and dying of Jesus may daily be more purified and renewed, against the day when Christ will present her to himself in all her glory, without spot.[1]

1 Samuel 8:4-22 warns us, however, to choose our solutions with care. When Samuel became old, his own sons began to take bribes and pervert justice.

> Then all the elders of Israel gathered together and said to Samuel, "You are old and your sons do not follow in your ways. Appoint for us, then, a king to govern us, like other nations."

God did not like the idea of a king. He said to Samuel, "They have not rejected you, but they have rejected me from being king over them." He then told Samuel to do what they wanted, but to warn them that human kings oppress:

> "In that day you will cry out because of your king, whom you have chosen for yourselves"... But the people refused to listen .... They said, "No! We are determined to have a king over us so that we also may be like other nations...."

When Church government is "like that of other nations" we are in trouble! Cardinal Leger, Archbishop of Montreal, said in the Vatican Council that the "splendor" of the "ornaments and titles which we [bishops] often use against our will... are harmful to our pastoral ministry," especially to the poor. "Perhaps this splendor was thought to be necessary when some bishops held secular authority as well. But in our time... such display is out of tune with our spirit."

Jesus gave "our spirit" when he said, "The rulers of the Gentiles lord it over them... It will not be so among you. Whoever wishes to be great among you must be your servant." We need to remain *aware* of the dignity God sees in us and accept no pretense of any other.[2]

In **Mark 2:1-12** Jesus said to those who doubted him: "that you may know that the Son of Man has authority on earth to forgive sins"—he said to the paralytic, "Stand up, take your mat and go home."

The only power the Church needs to project is the power to forgive. And to heal the afflicted. Then the whole world will *"sing the goodness of the Lord."*

---

[1] Decree on *Ecumenism*, no. 4. See also *Church in the Modern World*, no. 19; *Apostolate of the Laity*, nos. 3, 6, 10, 18, 25; *Catechism of the Catholic Church*, nos. 1913-1917; John Paul II, *Exhortation after the Synod on Reconciliation*, 1984, no. 16.

[2] *Council Speeches of Vatican II*, ed. Kung et al., Paulist Press, 1964, pp. 114-115; *Matthew* 20:25.

Response: Identify what affects your awareness. Make it speak truth.

January 14, 2012

Lord, your strength gives joy to the king.
(Responsorial: Psalm 21)

In **1 Samuel 9:1 to 10:1** God tells Samuel he has chosen Saul to be Israel's king:

> "You shall anoint him to be ruler over my people Israel. He shall save my people from the hand of the Philistines; for I have seen the suffering of my people."

When Samuel told Saul this, Saul had a hard time believing it. He answered:

> "My family is the humblest of all the families of the tribe of Benjamin. Why then have you spoken to me in this way?"

But Samuel anointed him anyway, as all of us were anointed at Baptism to continue the saving mission of Jesus as *Prophet*, *Priest*, and *King*:

> Samuel took a vial of oil and poured it on his head, and kissed him; he said, "The Lord has anointed you ruler over his people Israel. You shall reign over the people of the LORD and you will save them from the power of the enemies surrounding them."

Lines after the reading tell us:

> As Saul turned away to leave Samuel, God gave him another heart… and the spirit of God possessed him…. When all who knew him before saw how he prophesied with the prophets, the people said to one another, "What has come over the son of Kish? Is Saul also among the prophets?"

It is hard for us to believe, much less remain *aware*, that we have been chosen and anointed by God as truly as Saul was. And for an even greater mission: to be the body of Jesus himself acting *with* us, *in* us, and *through* us to save the people we deal with "from the power of the enemies surrounding them"—that is, from the "Philistines" of our society whose blindness distorts the attitudes and values of American culture.

God has given us "another heart" by Baptism: "If anyone is in Christ, there is a new creation: everything old has passed away; see, everything has become new!"

As *disciples* we have "become obedient from the heart to the form of teaching to which we were entrusted." As *prophets* we make evident through our lifestyle that "out of the believer's heart shall flow rivers of living water." As *priests* we "have unity of spirit, sympathy, love for one another, a tender heart, and a humble mind." And as stewards of Christ's *kingship* we know, "with the eyes of our heart enlightened, what is the hope to which he has called us, what are the riches of his glorious inheritance among the saints." With the awareness of this hope in our hearts we work to establish God's reign on earth "while we wait for the blessed hope and the manifestation of the glory of our great God and Savior, Jesus Christ."[1]

We have reason to sing, *"Lord, your strength gives joy to the king."*

God called Saul through Samuel. In **Mark 2:13-17** Jesus himself calls Levi to become Matthew the Apostle and Evangelist. And acting *with*, *in*, and *through* the minister of our Baptism, Jesus called us. We just have to keep ourselves *aware of the mystery* of our new identity and call.

[1] *2 Corinthians* 5:17. See *John* 7:38; *Romans* 6:17; *Ephesians* 1:18; *1 Peter* 3:8; *Titus* 2:13.

Response: Believe in your anointing. Keep yourself *aware* of what you are.

FOR REFLECTION AND DISCUSSION: EPIPHANY, FIRST WEEK IN ORDINARY TIME

Awareness of the Light: To be guided by the Light, we have to see and follow it.

Invitation: To focus on the Light.

For prayer and discussion: How many of these statements do you feel you understand? How often are you consciously aware of them?

Sunday: Before it can be seen, the light has to shine. "Preaching" the Good News means letting the glory of God's light in us shine out in all we are, say, and do. It is *we* who are the Epiphany.

The first thing we have to do, however, is cultivate *awareness*.

Monday: The essence of our redemption is that by Baptism we have "become Christ." The Father now says about each one of us what he said about Jesus: "This is my Son, my Daughter, the Beloved."

What we *choose* determines who we are more than what we accomplish.

Tuesday: Are we content to just pass through life like a pinball, without purpose or plan, bouncing haphazardly off of one experience after another, racking up random points until we fall at last into the slot that tallies up our final score?

Wednesday: The truth is, we do "know the Lord." We just may not be *aware* of it. We know him with the divine knowledge that comes with the gift of faith. But we will not be conscious of knowing him until we translate this into human knowledge by reading and reflecting on the human character of Jesus as revealed in the Scriptures. When we *express* our thoughts about him—to ourselves or others—in human words, that is when we realize we know him.

Thursday: The mystery of our being is that we have "become Christ." There simply is no dignity "higher" than that.

Friday: Too few people are aware that the bishops at Vatican II called on every Catholic to "undertake with vigor the task of renewal and reform" in response to abuses in the Church.

Saturday: God has given us "another heart" by Baptism.

Initiatives:
Form the habit of deliberately trying to express divine truth, life, love.
Put glasses of water where they will remind you of your Baptism. Bless yourself.
Write your name on a paper. Be aware you are writing it on your heart.
Say the WIT prayer all day long. Make all you do explicitly divine.
Know yourself as empowered by grace. Live as human and divine.
Remind yourself, when you show respect to anyone, that all are equal.
Identify what affects your awareness. Make it speak truth.
Believe in your anointing. Keep yourself *aware* of what you are.

Second Sunday in Ordinary Time — SUNDAY

January 15, 2012
We Are Called and Sent

Here am I, Lord. I come to do your will.
(Responsorial: Psalm 40)

INVENTORY

What is your most constant preoccupation? In being aware of that, what are you less aware of? What might you be losing sight of altogether?

INPUT

The *Entrance Antiphon* expresses the desire that "all the earth" will give God "worship and praise." We echo this every time we pray in the *Our Father*, "Hallowed be thy Name!" But concretely, how do we worship him? What do we praise him for? Are both a constant preoccupation?

The *Opening Prayer(s)* tell us that our Father "orders all things in such power that even the tensions and tragedies of sin cannot frustrate [his] loving plans." Not ultimately. But we know that often God's will is not done, and people block the good he desires to bring about. So we pray, "Help us to embrace your will." We are aware that for us God's will is that we should continue the mission of Jesus. So we add, "Give us the strength to follow your call," We ask this "so that your truth may live in our hearts," be seen in our actions, and "reflect peace" to all who, through what they see in us, will be helped to "believe in your love."

"HERE I AM"

In Chad, Africa, when a Ngama father names his son, he knows the name is just temporary. The boy will not receive his real name until he is initiated into full participation in the life of the tribe. This is also true of us.

The name parents give to their baby in the hospital, to be written on the birth certificate, is only the child's "citizen" name as an American. The child's real name as a child of God whose "citizenship is in heaven" will not be given until Baptism. It might be the same name in terms of the way it is spelled and pronounced. But it is not the same name at all. The new name is given by God, and its true meaning is known to God alone.[1]

In two of today's readings—**1 Samuel 3:3-19** and **John 1:35-42**—God is calling people by name. And also naming them by his call.

> The LORD called, "Samuel! Samuel!" and he said, "Here I am!" and ran to Eli [because] Samuel did not yet know the LORD, and the word of the LORD had not yet been revealed to him.

When God called Samuel's name, he also gave him his name as a prophet:

> As Samuel grew up, the LORD was with him …. And all Israel … came

SUNDAY SECOND SUNDAY IN ORDINARY TIME

to know that Samuel was accredited as a prophet of the Lord (verse 20).

When Andrew brought his brother Simon to Jesus, Jesus "looked at him and said, 'You are Simon son of John. You are to be called Cephas' (which is translated Peter)"—that is, the "Rock" on which Jesus would build his Church.

We don't need to hear God's voice calling us in the night, or to see Jesus telling us face-to-face that he has given us a "name"; that is, a special identity defined by our personal, unique relationship with him and by the distinctive role that each of us is called to play in continuing his mission on earth. The angels heard God's voice on the day of our Baptism, whether we heard it with our ears or not. And what they heard was God the Father calling us by name (and naming us by our call) as he said, "This is my beloved son, my precious daughter, whom I have chosen. As my Son Jesus was anointed for his messianic mission as Prophet, Priest and King, I anoint you to live and continue his mission as a member of his body."[2]

That is simply Catholic doctrine. If we had seen a vision and heard God's voice speaking to us, we might doubt whether it was real. But about what God said to us at Baptism there is no doubt. That is an article of faith.

We need to keep ourselves *aware* of it.

"DO YOU NOT KNOW…"

In **1 Corinthians 6:13-20** Paul asks three times: "Do you not know…?"

> Do you not know that your bodies are members of Christ? …
>
> Or do you not know that your body is a temple of the Holy Spirit within you, which you have from God, and that you are not your own?

Of course we know it. We were taught this as children. But that does not mean we understand it. Or that we are constantly *aware* of it.

Making—and keeping—ourselves *aware* of what we are, of what grace has made us and is calling us to be right now, this is the first phase of our conscious, explicit journey into the "perfection of love." Everything begins with the realization of our graced (divine) relationship with God. Until we can say with wonder and awe, "Our Father who art in heaven…." we have not entered with conscious understanding into the "grace of the Lord Jesus Christ." We have not *heard* the Good News. And if we are not *aware* of it we are forgetting it. And diminishing its benefits. So be aware!

[1]*Philippians* 3:20; *Ephesians* 2:19; *Hebrews* 13:14; *1 Peter* 2:9-16; *John* 14:1-3.
[2]*Matthew* 17:5; *Luke* 9:35. See the *Rite of Baptism* for children.

INSIGHT
What is your name? Who gave it to you? What does it mean? How can you find out?

INITIATIVE
Listen to what God is calling you to do. Find yourself in it.

SECOND WEEK IN ORDINARY TIME **MONDAY**

JANUARY 16, 2012

To the upright I will show the saving power of God.
(*Responsorial: Psalm 50*)

1 Samuel 15:16-23 makes it forcefully clear that the first and essential way to glorify God or "hallow" his Name is to do what he commands. The failure to do this is what gives religion a bad name.

When Saul attacked the Amalekites, God told him through Samuel to "utterly destroy all that they have; do not spare them, but kill both man and woman, child and infant, ox and sheep." But:

> Saul and the people spared the best of the sheep and cattle, and all that was valuable. All that was worthless they destroyed.

The Lord then said: "I regret that I made Saul king, for he has not carried out my commands." Confronted with this, Saul claimed he had obeyed, because he had used the best of what should have been destroyed to offer sacrifice to God—like someone who makes money by taking advantage of the poor and then gives a big donation to the Church.

> Samuel said, "Is the pleasure of the Lord in burnt offerings and sacrifices, or in obedience to the voice of the Lord? Yes, obedience is better than sacrifices."

Scripture scholars tell us not to take literally the command to kill men, women, and children. The God who spoke to Samuel is the same God who said in the second Vatican Council:

> Any act of war aimed indiscriminately at the destruction of entire cities… along with their population is a crime against God and humanity itself. It deserves unequivocal and unhesitating condemnation.

The point 1 Samuel makes is that, if we see God and creatures in perspective with authentic *"Fear of the Lord,"* nothing—absolutely no created value—takes precedence over the will of God. And no human act, nothing we "give" to God, including all the prayers and worship in the world, can substitute for living the way God commands.

That command, from beginning to end, is love. If we do not love God and neighbor—and show it in actions—nothing "religious" we do is authentic.

> So when you are offering your gift at the altar, if you remember that your brother or sister has something against you, leave your gift there before the altar and go; first be reconciled to your brother or sister.

We all know this. But we need to keep ourselves *aware* of it. How many people come untroubled to Mass though they speak with consistent venom about the President, politicians, and members of the Church they consider "unorthodox"? Haters cannot present themselves as "acceptable sacrifices" to God.[1]

In **Mark 2:18-22** Jesus calls us to be aware of what we are actually *expressing* in our religious acts. Fasting is a physical expression of spiritual hunger for union with the Bridegroom. If not, it has little spiritual value. Or at least, not the value that fasting, prayer, and all other religious acts should take on now that Jesus has poured out the "new wine" of mystery into our hearts.

---

[1] *The Church Today*, no. 80. *Matthew* 5:23-24; *Romans* 12:1.

Response: Be aware of who God is and of who you are. Live mystery.

TUESDAY SECOND WEEK IN ORDINARY TIME

JANUARY 17, 2012

I have found David my servant.
(Responsorial: Psalm 89)

1 Samuel 16:1-13 tells how God chose David to replace Saul, to whom Samuel said that, had he obeyed, "The LORD would have established your kingdom over Israel forever." But God called David "a man after his own heart," and never rejected him. Why?

David raped the wife of a faithful officer, and ordered him murdered in a shameful way to cover up his crime. Was Saul's sin worse than that?[1]

David broke God's law in a way that was horrible. But he did it out of passion and weakness. He abused his power like most kings did. But he did not go against God's personal, direct command to him; while Saul disobeyed in a way Samuel called "rebellion" and "no less a sin than divination" or idolatry. "Because you have rejected the word of the LORD, he has also rejected you from being king."

We have to ask two things about sin; what it does to others, and what it does to us. What it does to us is determined mostly by what it *expresses*. By doing this, what am I saying (and therefore making real) about my relationship with others? And above all, with God?

Who I am, my personal identity, is determined by the choices that establish the *relationships* I choose to maintain with God, other people, and the rest of creation. In that order. The relationships I choose define me as a person. By every choice I augment or diminish, am faithful or false to, some relationship.

Life-determining acts, good or bad, are those which express the choice, conscious or not, to maintain or destroy the relationship I have with another. Sins that destroy our graced relationship with God are called "mortal." They include sins that destroy the fundamental relationship of love God calls us to have with other people. The two essential commandments are:

> "You shall love the Lord your God with all your heart, and with all your soul, and with all your mind." This is the greatest and first commandment. And a second is like it: "You shall love your neighbor as yourself." On these two commandments hang all the law and the prophets.

Every temptation faces me with the choice to love or not to love.[2]

In **Mark 2:23-28** all the Pharisees saw was Jesus' disciples "doing what is not lawful on the Sabbath." Jesus saw hungry men feeding themselves. The "law-observance" mentality, now as well as then, does not ask what is beneficial or harmful to individuals in particular cases. For Pharisees there are no particular cases; just the LAW: as unchanging and absolute as God. In practice, the LAW is their God.

When Jesus said, "The Sabbath was made for humankind, not humankind for the Sabbath," he taught that to keep God's laws we have to start by asking what is good for people; what is love.

[1] See *1 Samuel* 13:13-14; *2 Samuel*, chapter 11.
[2] *Matthew* 22:36-40.

Response: Do God's will in keeping his laws. Do the loving thing.

Second Week in Ordinary Time Wednesday

January 18, 2012

Blessed be the Lord, my rock.
(*Responsorial: Psalm* 144)

In **1 Samuel 17:32-51** young David brings down the giant Goliath with a slingshot. But the heart of the story is the difference between what Goliath was *aware* of and what David was.

Goliath was just aware of what he saw: his size and strength compared to David's, his weapons compared to David's. David was aware of something not seen: the mystery of God's presence, God's involvement in the fight, and of himself as aided by God's strength.

We can't help seeing in the "five stones" David picked up out of the water of the riverbed something not intended by Scripture but still true: the five "weapons" God gives us in Baptism to help us "meet and defeat" life's challenges, even the most gigantic. These five "weapons" (5 phrases and 5 phases) are reflected in the Our Father.

The first is *awareness of our identity* as children of the Father. We "pick up" this stone every time we make ourselves *aware* of *"Our Father… in heaven!"* and of his divine life in us.

The second is *enlightenment*. We "pick up" this stone when we *commit* to the prayerful study of God that makes us able to "glorify" or *"hallow" his Name*.

The third is the *power* of the Holy Spirit that we begin to use when we *dedicate* ourselves to making his *Kingdom come*, beginning with a lifestyle that accredits us as *prophetic witnesses* to Christ.

The fourth stone is God's promise that we will have a *posterity* by giving life to others through priestly ministry. We pick it up when we *surrender* to letting the Father's *will be done* in us and through us by Christ expressing his truth and love in our words and actions.

The fifth stone is the sustaining assurance of *victory* in our efforts, as *stewards of his kingship*, to establish God's reign over all creation. We pick it up as we *abandon ourselves* to an all-consuming hunger for the *daily Bread* of Christ given in the "wedding banquet of the Lamb" to all who are *forgiving as they are forgiven* in the "unity and peace of his kingdom."

With these five stones, taken from the waters of Baptism, we can meet and defeat any enemy that comes against us.

Mark 3:1-6 continues yesterday's teaching. In the synagogue was a man with a withered hand. The Pharisees of the "law and order" party were watching "to see whether Jesus would cure him on the Sabbath, so that they might accuse him." They didn't care about the man's suffering. All they cared about was law observance. We find this today.

Jesus asked them: "Is it keeping God's law to do good on the Sabbath, or to do harm? To save life or to kill?"

They wouldn't answer him. "They were silent." Every priest who has ever been accused of breaking rules by "legalists" in the Church knows that, if he explains the pastoral justification for what he did, they will simply "be silent." They are not interested in truth, just laws. When they did this to Jesus, he "looked around at them with anger." It is the only time he ever did.

Response: Keep aware of the mystery of divine life. Do not become a nitpicker.

THURSDAY SECOND WEEK IN ORDINARY TIME

JANUARY 19, 2012

In God I trust; I shall not fear.
(Responsorial: Psalm 56)

In **1 Samuel 18:6 to 19:7** envy of David's popularity makes Saul decide to kill him. This was really stupid. What had he ceased to be *aware* of?

Saul had forgotten he was only king by obedience: because God told him to be. Without God's support, what was he?

He was ignoring the gift of *Fear of the Lord*, which would have shown him that, seen in perspective, the real value of his kingship was in the *relationship* he had with the Infinite God who had chosen and anointed him. To give up this relationship with the All Good, All Loving One for the sake of the limited benefits of earthly rule was idiocy. And to try to defeat God the All Mighty by killing David was insanity.

He was also ignoring *Wisdom*, the gift of "taste" for spiritual things, joined to the habit of seeing everything in the light of the "last end." Saul first found joy in his kingship because he was being obedient to God, serving God, pleasing God. But gradually he became less aware of this spiritual joy and more conscious of the perks, popularity, prestige and power he found in palace life on a throne. Then he shortened his focus to the here-and-now and lost sight of the final goal: union with the Eternal God. He lost *Wisdom*. Became *unaware*.

Mark 3:7-12: The "Pharisee party" is strong in the Church and always will be. But more numerous are all the good people who come to Jesus honestly, but for the wrong reason.

A great multitude followed him... for he had cured many, so that all who had diseases pressed upon him to touch him.

They came, not primarily to learn from Jesus or to become holy, but because they were suffering and hoped he would heal them. Like people today who come to church for relief, strength to face the ordinary challenges of life, with some hope it will make them "feel good." Which is legitimate. And good.

Those who came to Jesus to be healed had *faith* that he could, *hope* that he would, and *love* for the God who showed in Jesus that he cared for them. They just didn't want, or even think about, what Jesus came to give; "life to the full," the "eternal life," that is to *know the Father*, "the only true God, and Jesus Christ whom he has sent." This is true of most Christians still.[1]

Wisdom (as defined above) is rare. *Fear of the Lord* moves people to do what they have to do to "get to heaven," but not much more. The perspective that shows God as All that is good, and everything else as nothing in comparison, is lacking. Bottom line: mediocrity.

That is why Jesus "ordered the demons not to make him known." He did not want people who came for healing to identify this as the role of the Messiah. He longed to tell them, "You will see greater things than these." But they weren't ready to hear it. Are you?[2]

[1] *John* 10:10; 17:3.
[2] See *John* 1:50.

Response: Write down what you want to "get out of" religion. Grade yourself.

JANUARY 20, 2012

Have mercy on me, God, have mercy.
(Responsorial: Psalm 57)

1 Samuel 24:3-21 shows us a contrast in *awareness*. Saul was intent on killing David, his focus limited to only one thing: David was a threat to his position and power. When Saul came alone into the cave where David and his men were hiding, and did not see them, all his men could think of was, "This is our chance to kill him." But David was keenly aware of something else: "He is the anointed of the Lord." David felt guilty for even cutting off quietly a corner of Saul's cloak, so he could show him later that he could have killed him and didn't. This is called *Fear of the Lord*: not fright, but overwhelming respect for the awesome majesty and goodness of God and for everything and everyone connected to him.

By the same perspective David saw himself, and said Saul should see him, as having no more importance than a "dead dog" or a "single flea." What was David, or what is anyone, if we ignore our relationship with God? Except for God's present, continuing choice to keep us in existence, of ourselves we are simply nothing. We would drop into non-being. But if we make a point of always seeing people—ourselves and others—in the light of the relationship each has with God, whatever it may be, we will always respect others as we respect God. This is true *Fear of the Lord*.

It is also *Wisdom*: seeing everything in the light of the "last end." We know the true "mystery of God's will," that he "set forth in Christ, as a plan for the fullness of time." It is to "*bring all things in the heavens and on earth into one under Christ's headship*." All things in heaven and on earth will be "united," "gathered up," "summed up," "recapitulated," "brought together under a single Head." This is Paul's vision of the radiant glory, shrouded in mystery, of the "end time."[1]

How will we treat each other now if we keep aware of how we will be seeing and loving each other while sharing the Bread of the "wedding banquet of the Lamb," when God will be forgiving us all as we forgive each other?

Mark 3:13-19: Jesus "called to him those whom he wanted...."

> And he appointed twelve; they were to be his companions, and to be sent out to proclaim the message, with power to cast out demons.

The Twelve named in the Gospel were chosen as unique witnesses to the Resurrection because, as Peter said later when the community replaced Judas, they were present "during all the time that the Lord Jesus went in and out among us, beginning from the baptism of John until the day when he was taken up from us." But "apostle" just means "sent," and every one of us is "sent" by our "messianic anointing" at Baptism as *prophet, priest,* and *king*. We just have to keep ourselves *aware* of it.[2]

[1] *Ephesians* 1:10; *Colossians* 1:16.
[2] *Acts* 1:15-26; *Romans* 16:7; *1 Corinthians* 4:9; *Ephesians* 4:11.

Response: Never forget to be aware of everyone's relationship with God.

Saturday Second Week in Ordinary Time

January 21, 2012

Let us see your face, Lord, and we shall be saved.
(Responsorial: Psalm 80)

Because of Saul's mood swings, some Scripture scholars have speculated that he was bi-polar. If he was, it was irrelevant to David, who never for an instant forgot that Saul was God's anointed. That was how he saw him and how he treated him.

Today's reading, taken from **2 Samuel 1:1-27**, omits the verses that tell how Saul's death was reported. The messenger said Saul thought he was mortally wounded and had asked him to kill him, so he did. But David said, "Were you not afraid to lift your hand to destroy the Lord's anointed?" And he had the messenger executed.

Then David sang of Saul, and of Jonathan, who died in the same battle:

> Saul and Jonathan, loved and lovely, neither in life nor in death were divided. Swifter than eagles were they, stronger were they than lions.
>
> O daughters of Israel, weep for Saul, who clothed you in scarlet and fine linen, who set brooches of gold on your garments. How did the heroes fall…?

This is how David remembered Saul, who did everything he could to kill him. And this is the kind of awareness we should cultivate in our thoughts about every person we deal with. This is the kind of respect that grows out of authentic *Fear of the Lord*.

Mark 3:20-21 tells us that at times Jesus' own family thought he was crazy:

> He went home; and such a crowd collected that they could not even have a meal.
>
> When his relatives heard of this, they set out to take charge of him, convinced he was out of his mind.

To be "out of you mind" means to be out of touch with reality. But you might look the same way if you are *in touch* with more reality than "normal" people are aware of. Those who are aware of the mystery of God; of God's relationship with the world and of our relationship with him; of the awesome reality of grace making us and others authentic children of God and sharers in his divine life, do not relate to anything or anyone in this world in a way that is "normal" in our culture. This is the essence of Christian *witness*: to live a lifestyle that raises questions because it raises eyebrows.

If we are really in touch with the Good News, aware of the new *identity*, the *enlightenment*, the *power*, the *"posterity"* (fruitful ministry) and *victory* promised to those who really believe in Jesus Christ, how can we not be so obsessed by the need to share that with others that even our friends and family sometimes wonder if we are out of our mind?

This is what happened to Jesus.

It is mostly a question of *awareness*. "Let us see your face, Lord—constantly—and we shall be saved." And save others.

Response: Cultivate awareness. Say the WIT prayer all day long. Read Scripture.

FOR REFLECTION AND DISCUSSION: SECOND WEEK IN ORDINARY TIME

We Are Called and Sent: God knows us by name and calls us to mission.

Invitation: To focus on the explicitness of our call and our response.

For prayer and discussion: How many of these statements do you feel you understand? How often are you consciously aware of them?

Sunday: Making—and keeping—ourselves *aware* of what we are, of what grace has made us and is calling us to be right now, this is the first phase of our conscious, explicit journey into the "perfection of love." Everything begins with the realization of our graced (divine) relationship with God that enables us to say with wonder and awe, *"Our Father who art in heaven…."*

Monday: …no human act, nothing we "give" to God, including all the prayers and worship in the world, can substitute for living the way God commands.

Tuesday: *Who* I am, my personal identity, is determined by the choices that establish the *relationships* I choose to maintain with God, other people and the rest of creation. In that order. By every choice I augment or diminish, am faithful or false to, some relationship.

Wednesday: David was aware of something not seen: the mystery of God's presence, God's involvement in his life, and of himself as aided by God's strength.

Thursday: Saul first found joy in his kingship because he was being obedient to God, serving God, pleasing God. But gradually he became more conscious of the perks, the popularity, prestige, and power. Then he shortened his focus to the here-and-now and lost sight of the final goal: union with the Eternal God. He lost *Wisdom*. Became *unaware*.

Friday: If we make a point of always seeing people—ourselves and others—in the light of the relationship each has with God, whatever it may be, we will always respect others as we respect God. This is true *Fear of the Lord*.

Saturday: If we are really in touch with the Good News, aware of the new *identity*, the *enlightenment*, the *power*, the "*posterity*" (fruitful ministry) and *victory* promised, how can we not be obsessed by the need to share that with others?

Initiatives:
Listen to what God is calling you to do. Find yourself in it.
Be aware of who God is and of who you are. Live mystery.
Do God's will in keeping his laws. Do the loving thing.
Keep aware of the mystery of divine life. Do not become a nitpicker.
Write down what you want to "get out of" religion. Grade yourself.
Never forget to be aware of everyone's relationship with God.
Cultivate awareness. Say the WIT prayer all day long. Read Scripture.

SUNDAY Third Sunday in Ordinary Time

January 22, 2012
The Power of Light and Love

Teach me yours ways, O Lord.
(Responsorial: Psalm 25)

Inventory

How much power do you think you have? Who has more real power: presidents or parents? Priests or peers? What can each do?

Input

The *Entrance Antiphon* calls us to *"sing a new song to the Lord,"* A new song doesn't do any good unless someone is singing it. Singing to the Lord is always good. But singing where there is nobody around to hear doesn't help other people much. So the antiphon continues: "Sing to the Lord *all the earth*!" We want to make the "new song" of Christianity the song of the whole human race.

In the *Opening Prayer* we ask God to "direct *your love that is within us* so that our efforts in the name of your Son may bring humanity to unity and peace." The power to do this is love. And that love is within us. It is God's love. We share in it.

In the alternate *Opening Prayer* we ask "that the *limits* of our faults and weaknesses may *not obscure the vision* of your glory." Whatever "limits" the scope of our awareness by focusing us on the things of this world "obscures the vision" of the mystery revealed to us: the Good News of the *new identity* we have by grace; of the *enlightenment* we grow into through God's word; of the *power to bear witness* that is ours through the Gift of the Holy Spirit; of the *posterity* promised us if we will mediate the life of God to others through ministry; of the *victory* that will crown our efforts to establish the reign of God over every area and activity of human life. We need to keep the vision clear, to keep ourselves *aware* of the "new song," the new relationship with God made possible by Jesus Christ for those who are "in him."

In the *Prayer after Communion* we ask: "May the *new life* you give us *increase* our love…." Christian life on earth is all about growth: growth into clearer light through faith, stronger encouragement through hope, more generous efforts through love. And growth begins with *awareness* of the mystery of God: *"Truth and beauty surround him. He lives in holiness and glory."* This is our "new song."

The People Believed

In **Jonah 3:1-10** there are five things to notice: 1. Jonah "went to Nineveh in obedience to the word of the Lord." It wasn't his idea or personal project. In fact, he didn't want to do it (read the first two chapters). So when he did, he was very *aware* that he was preaching as an instrument of God and that God was speaking in him and through him. 2. "The people of Nineveh *believed*." They took God's words seriously. 3. They *did something* about it. "They proclaimed a fast and put on sackcloth, from the greatest to the least." 4. This was a *communal* response. They expressed themselves as a community. No exceptions. The king himself "covered himself with sackcloth, and sat in ashes." 5. "God relented." Their response saved the city from disaster.

This encourages us to believe that, not only individuals, but families, the Church, even entire nations, can be converted from the distortions and spiritual mediocrity that are destroying them. But someone has to call them to it as a *prophet* delivering God's message. And they have to *believe*, *reflect* on God's words *together* as *disciples*, and *respond* as a united community, each taking *responsibility* as *priest* and *king*.

Are you *aware* that you were consecrated by God at Baptism to be a *prophet*? To deliver God's message to all you live and work with? Is your community—family, circle of friends or associates, your parish—aware of itself as a community of faith, called to reflect on God's words together in order to come to decisions that embody a communal response? What are you doing to make them (and yourself) aware of this?

"Follow Me and I...."

You may be asking, "Who am I to convert my family to anything? Or my friends? Or my parish?" The truth is, most families are not *aware* of themselves as communities of faith. And even parishes do not engage in much communal discussion about how they should live out, express or grow in the faith they share. It is possible, even commonplace, for people to share the same faith without sharing it with each other. This leads to disaster.

Mark 1:14-20 should encourage us. Who were these men Jesus chose to convert the world? They were ordinary, family-business fishermen. The four in this Gospel probably couldn't read and write. Peter, who wound up pope, had more recorded sins and errors than anyone else in the four Gospels. The others must have thought it a joke when Jesus re-named him "the Rock." But he turned out to be a rock. A rock of human shortsightedness and weakness held together by the grace of God.[1]

Jonah wasn't so holy either. He literally ran away from what God wanted him to do. It took a "whale of a lesson" to turn him around. (Sorry). Does God have to feed you to the fish to get you to carry a message to your family, friends, and parish? Or, if you refuse, is he just going to let you go down with them?

We all need to keep *aware*—because God is going to judge us on it—that we have an official job to do, a call and commissioning from God we cannot deny. Like it or not, we *are* consecrated to continue Christ's mission as *Prophet*, *Priest*, and *King*; that is, to let him continue it in us. "Follow me," he says, "and *I will make you* fishers of people." He is telling us what *he* will do in us and through us—if we stay aware of it.

The Greatest Power

What is the greatest power on earth? Authorities and lawmakers have power to affect or change peoples' actions. It takes a greater power to change peo-

SUNDAY THIRD SUNDAY IN ORDINARY TIME

ples' hearts. And that, more than anything else, is the power of *example*.

Who are children more likely to imitate? The President or their parents? Whose attitudes and values are teenagers more likely to adopt? Those preached from the pulpit or those they see lived-out in their peer group? Children will participate in Mass the way their parents do; or believe, at least, that is how they should. More powerful, perhaps, than the example of parents, is what they see and hear their brothers and sisters doing. Praying, cursing, obeying, smoking, helping others, drinking, reading the Bible, driving recklessly, watching clean TV or porn—we embrace these things because of others' example. Others' power.

St. Paul uses the phrase "should live" in almost every one of the few sentences of **1 Corinthians 7:29-31**. He is telling us how people who know that "the time is growing short" *should live* in order to help each other be *aware* that all the joys and sufferings, all the professions and preoccupations of this world, important as they might be, are passing away even as we engage in them. With the enlightened sense of perspective we enjoy through *Fear of the Lord*, nothing we deal with in our culture should have power to scare us or seduce us, put us under pressure, or throw us off guard. Why? Because "the world as we know it is *passing away*."

Hearing this from the pulpit can help us somewhat to be free. Talking about it with each other might help more. But what Paul counts on to help Christians really *believe* that we are free from the fears and slavery others experience (free from all fears that are not *Fear of the Lord*) is the support we give each other by our *example*. The married who visibly *live* as couples invited to the "wedding banquet of the Lamb"; the bereaved who visibly *live* as people who know they are only separated for a time from their loved ones; those who "enjoy the good things of this world" but visibly *live* in a way that shows they aren't attached to them; those "whose life is buying things," whether professionally or for private use, who *live* in a way that makes it evident possessions have little importance for them; and those who "have to deal with the world" who visibly *live* as if they were hardly affected by it—these are the people who help themselves and others remain *aware* of the Good News. By their *example* they are the most powerful people on earth.

[1] Peter was wrong when: he rejected Jesus' way of saving the world; (*Matthew* 16:22); he misunderstood what the transfiguration meant (17:4); he presumed Jesus would pay the temple tax (17:25); he objected to Jesus' washing his feet (*John* 16:22); he protested that he would never deny Jesus (*Matthew* 26:35); he slept during Jesus' agony in the garden (Jesus singled him out by name in his reproach: *Matthew* 26:40); he opted for violence and cut off Malchus' ear when Jesus was arrested (*John* 18:10).

INSIGHT
Has this refection made power *something you want to think about in your life?*

INITIATIVE
Write down all you started doing because of others' example. Look twice.

Third Week in Ordinary Time MONNDAY

January 23, 2012

My faithfulness and love shall be with him.
(Responsorial: Psalm 89)

In **2 Samuel 5:1-10** the people give power to David.

> "The LORD said to you: It is you who shall… be ruler over Israel." So all the elders… anointed David king over Israel.

They did it because they knew the Lord had chosen him. This is the only real and legitimate source of authority.

We obey authorities because they are over us in our employment, or elected officials, or sometimes because, literally or not, they are "holding a gun to our head." We don't need to believe they were chosen by God. To obey as Christians, however, we do need to believe God wants us to obey them; even if as the lesser of two evils; for example, so we won't lose a job in which, in spite of the power structure, we are able to do some good.

The point is, there is peace in this. It is stressful and unhealthy to be working while, the whole time, a voice inside us is saying, "I shouldn't have to be doing this!" That is to live with inner conflict. But everything changes if we say, "This is stupid," or unjust, "but I know that, under the circumstances, it is what God wants me to do now. Thy will be done."

This is the way Jesus went to the cross.

Just to keep ourselves *aware*, that in the last analysis we are obeying God—doing God's will even in surrendering to something that in itself is not God's will—this is what changes our burden into our cross; our frustration into fulfillment. True fulfillment is found, always and only, in doing God's will. If we can be satisfied that God wants us to endure what we are enduring, even if God hates it more than we do, we can find peace. There is no stress in surrender. But we have to keep ourselves *aware* of *whom* we are obeying. Our obedience is worship. Always.[1]

Mark 3:22-30 approaches this from another angle. The "scribes" did not accept Jesus as an authority. They said, "Beelzebul is in him," and "He casts out devils through the prince of devils."

Not all authorities are idiots and tyrants. Some, perhaps the great majority, really are chosen by God; at least in the sense that, however they were appointed, God accepts them and tries to work through them. Normally we should presume this, and presume they also are trying to hear and follow God's voice. But the scribes wouldn't do this. Not even for Jesus.

Far worse than not being able to surrender to God through a tyrant is not being *willing* to surrender to God through onc he has sent. If we reject people in whom the Spirit is speaking, Jesus says this can be to "blaspheme against the Holy Spirit." We may not like the message, but we should think twice before making rash accusations against the messenger. It may be God.

---

[1] Reflect on *Matthew* 28:18; *Luke* 4:6; 7:8; 12:5; *Acts* 5:29; *Romans* 13:1-8; *Ephesians* 1:17 to 2:3; *1 Peter* 2:9-21; *Revelation* 20:4.

Response: Look always for signs of God's presence before you reject anyone.

TUESDAY Third Week in Ordinary Time

JANUARY 24, 2012

Who is this king of glory?
It is the Lord.
(*Responsorial: Psalm* 24)

In **2 Samuel 6:12-19** David made a fool of himself in the eyes of his wife Michal, Saul's daughter. They were bringing the Ark of the Covenant into the city, and David was dancing, "whirling around before the Lord with all his might, wearing nothing but a linen loincloth." Michal "despised him in her heart" and told him sarcastically:

> "How the king of Israel honored himself today, showing himself half naked before the eyes of his servants' maids, as if he were a nobody!"

David answered, "I was dancing in the presence of the Lord who chose me… as prince over Israel, his people. I will do it again, and humble myself even more."

There was a difference of *awareness* here. Michal was conscious of how David might look to other people. David thought only of how he looked to the Lord. Michal was wrapped up in her own dignity, while David had thrown his off together with his clothes. Michal wanted David to be more aware of himself as king. David was aware that everything he was came from God. He was filled with gratitude and appreciation. He simply couldn't say "Hallowed be thy Name" in a moderate tone of voice, standing still.

If we let ourselves be *aware* of what God is, we will be impelled to express what we feel. If we do not express it, or express it only in ways that "damn with faint praise," pretty soon we won't feel it anymore. Michal was too self-conscious, instead of God-conscious, to "let go." Her punishment (from God or from David?) was, "she had no child to the day of her death." To give God's life to others, we have to be so *aware* we are alive that it overflows. In self-expression. *Who is this king of glory? It is the Lord.* To see it we have to say it.

Mark 3:31-35 continues Saturday's account of how Jesus' family thought he was "out of his mind" because he would not stop preaching even to eat. Now the crowd tells him, "Your mother and your brothers and sisters are outside, asking for you." To which Jesus replied, "Who are my mother and my brothers?"

> And looking at those who sat around him, he said, "Here are my mother and my brothers! Whoever does the will of God is my brother and sister and mother!"

He was really carried away! But he meant it.

If Mary had been like Michal, when Jesus finally did come in for supper, she would have told him: "I threw it away. Go get one of your other 'brothers and sisters and mothers' to feed you!"

Mary might have said this anyway. After all, she was a real Jewish mother. But then she would have stuffed him full, because she shared his enthusiasm.

If we are never so carried away that we "lose ourselves" in praising God, something is lacking in our awareness of who God is and how he has brought us into relationship with himself. And if we don't *let* ourselves be carried away, we will never be fully aware of it.

Response: Drop your reserves. Express physically what you feel about God.

Feast of the Conversion of Saint Paul, Apostle — Wednesday

January 25, 2012

"Go out to all the world and tell the Good News."
(Responsorial: Mark 16:15; Psalm 117)

Acts 22:3-16 is Paul's basic experience of Jesus. It gives the key to everything he preached and wrote for the rest of his life. The Jesus Paul met, the Jesus he was aware of from that minute forward, was Jesus *identified with those who believe in him.*

When Paul asked, "Who are you?" Jesus answered, "I am Jesus of Nazareth *whom you are persecuting."* Paul could have responded, "I am persecuting your followers, not you." But he knew better. What he saw, what God gave him to understand from that moment, and what he never lost sight of, is that those who believe in Jesus have *become Christ* and he has become what they are.

Every one of us must identify ourselves as Paul identified himself: " It is no longer I who live, but it is Christ who lives in me."

This was the core of Paul's preaching: "the mystery hidden throughout the ages but now been revealed to his saints." Through Paul "God chose to make known how great among the Gentiles are the riches... of this mystery." And the mystery, the message Paul was sent to give to the world, is simply this: "*Christ in you*, the hope of glory."[1]

This was Paul's ministry: to *bring Christ to be* in all who accepted him: "My little children, for whom I am again in the pain of childbirth until Christ is formed in you." For Paul the "work of ministry" consisted in "building up the body of Christ," helping all grow "to maturity, to the measure of the full stature of Christ." More precisely, the goal is the *mystery of Christ* coming to perfection in us and we in him: "to make every person complete *in Christ*"—until we *"form that perfect man* who is *Christ come to full stature."*[2]

The first and foundational phase of our spiritual growth into the fullness of faith and knowledge, into maturity and the "perfection of love," is simply to cultivate *awareness* of the mystery of our new identity. This is the mystery of *Christ in us,* the "hope" and foretaste of the "glory" which is ours now and will be ours in its fullness when Christ has grown to "full stature" in us, the glorified Church, which is "*his body*, the fullness of him who fills all in all." Then we will truly "know the love of Christ that surpasses knowledge," and "be filled with all the fullness of God."

But the first step, the first phase, is to keep ourselves *aware* of who we are. **Mark 16:15-18:** Jesus sent, not just the Apostles, but all of us to "proclaim the Good News." We have to keep ourselves *aware* of this to do it.

[1]*Galatians* 2:20; *Colossians* 1:25-27.
[2]*Galatians* 4:19; *Ephesians* 4:11-13. See the 1970 New Testament of *The New American Bible.* The point of focus here in the Greek text is the *andra teleion*, Christ himself, head and members. Other translations have subtly shifted the focus to our growth rather than the mystery of Christ himself as the fulfillment of all creation. See also *Ephesians* 1:3-10; *Colossians* 1:9-20.

Response: Cultivate your true self-image. Say the WIT prayer all day long.

THURSDAY: THIRD WEEK IN ORDINARY TIME

JANUARY 26, 2012

God will give him the throne of David his Father.
(*Responsorial: Psalm* 132)

2 Samuel 7:18-29: There is something very interesting in David's response to God's promise. His focus is not on what it meant to himself, but on what it says about God:

> According to your own heart, you have wrought all this greatness, so that your servant may know it. Therefore you are great, O LORD God; for there is no one like you, and there is no God besides you....
>
> Thus your name will be magnified forever in the saying, "The LORD of hosts is God over Israel."

It is natural for a child who receives a present to say, "Thank you," then run off and get absorbed in the present. But David was absorbed in what the gift said about God. What he was most grateful for was the *relationship* God chose to have with him. This is what he was most *aware* of. And so he just kept thanking and praising God.

God overwhelms us with gifts: earth, air, food, water, flowers, trees, animals, fish, and birds. The gifts of grace: a new identity purified of sin, divine light, the power of the Holy Spirit, his word, instant access to himself in prayer, the Mass, the sacraments, a library of Christian reflections, and records of mystical experience, the example of the saints, community with others, the promise of life-giving ministry, and of a contributing part in establishing the reign of God on earth. But his greatest gift is the gift he wants to give us *through* these, the gift these other gifts help us to arrive at; the gift Jesus said he came to give: that "life to the full" which consists in being *like God*.

Not just "in the image" of God. Not just somewhat like God. Not just creatures imitating God to the best of our ability. God created us to "become Christ" by Baptism. To become "in Christ" what Jesus himself is, in a way "far more than all we can ask or imagine": the "reflection of God's glory and the exact imprint of God's very being." By "presenting our bodies as a living sacrifice" at Baptism to be his body, and reaffirming this at every Mass, we are accepting to be absorbed in Christ, so united to him that we can say with St. Paul: "It is no longer I who live, but it is Christ who lives in me!" Jesus' prayer for his disciples was not, "Father, may they be like us," but "may all be *one*. As *you, Father, are in me and I am in you*, may they also be *in us*."[1]

That is the mystery we need to remain *aware* of.

Mark 4:21-25: It is the nature of God to love, to give himself. If we are like God, we must be giving to others, sharing with others, all that we are. Jesus says,

> "Is a lamp brought in to be put… under the bed, and not on the lampstand? For there is nothing hidden, except to be disclosed; nor is anything secret, except to come to light.
>
> Let anyone with ears to hear listen!"

We will *be* like God in the measure we *give* like God. Our light and our love.

[1] *John* 10:10; *Hebrews* 1:3; *Ephesians* 3:20; *Romans* 12:1; *Galatians* 2:20; *John* 17:21.

Response: Be aware of God's gift. Share it. Sharing will keep you aware.

Third Week in Ordinary Time — Friday

January 27, 2012

*Be merciful, O Lord,
for we have sinned.*
(*Responsorial: Psalm* 51)

In **2 Samuel 11:1-17** David hit bottom. His sin was not only adultery but rape, because when he summoned to his palace the wife of Uriah, one of his faithful officers deployed in battle, she couldn't refuse. When she became pregnant, and David realized he couldn't hide from Uriah what he had done, he covered up his sin by having the army set up Uriah to die in battle. In this David was utterly contemptible.

And this is the man about whom God said, "I have found David… to be a man after my heart, who will carry out all my wishes." How do we explain this?[1]

First, we have to admit that we don't have the slightest idea of what the words "steadfast love" mean—the "virtual definition of God" in the Old Testament—until we see the unimaginable "kindness and fidelity" (same words) God shows to his friends.

More specific to David's case, however, is that God doesn't narrow his focus the way we do. We characterize someone as "a murderer" or "a liar" or, during wars, as "an enemy," and forget that no human can be reduced to just one element of being. How many wars would start or continue if every politician and soldier was acutely conscious that every "enemy" is a child of God? Or just a whole human being with good and bad points like every other? How many people would we execute as "criminals," if we didn't forget every thing else they are?

And how many people would leave the Church if they could not use the excuse of seeing just the sinners in the Church and not the saints? There is good and bad all through the Church, from the center, where clergy and laity live and work on ground level, all the way out through the bishops to the popes on the fringes. We need to keep ourselves *aware* of this and open our eyes.

Mark 4:26-34: To explain the growth of divine life in individuals and in the Church, Jesus says it is "as if someone would scatter seed on the ground, and would sleep and rise night and day, and the seed would sprout and grow, he does not know how." We don't know what is happening in peoples' hearts; we just know that God never stops working on people and in people according to his "steadfast love." He never gives up on anyone, and neither should we.

Or on the Church. If God could say to David, knowing how he would sin, "Your house and your kingdom shall be made sure forever before me; your throne shall be established forever," how much more sure are we that God will continue to live and work within his sinful Church? We need to keep the same "steadfast love" for the Church and for every person on earth that God does. God's life may look like a mustard seed now; but it grows. We need to keep ourselves *aware* of that. *Be merciful, O Lord, for we have sinned* speaks hope.

[1] *Acts* 13:22. Cf. *Psalm* 89:20 and *1 Kings* 14:8.

Response: Don't judge anyone with partial vision. See all with God's eyes.

Saturday Third Week in Ordinary Time

January 28, 2012

Create a clean heart in me, O Lord.
(Responsorial: Psalm 51)

2 Samuel 12:1-17 makes one thing clear to us; we don't know anyone else's deepest heart, and often not our own.

When Nathan confronted David with his sin, what David revealed was that he despised what he had done. He wasn't aware he was speaking of himself when he said, "As the LORD lives, the man who has done this deserves to die… because he had no pity." But when Nathan made him aware, he said, "I have sinned against the LORD."

With those words David discovered his heart.

It is hard to sin with full consciousness of what we are doing. We block out a lot. Afterwards, if we feel guilt and remorse, we are usually blocking out something else: we are judging ourselves by our actions without asking how authentically those actions reveal our heart, our true selves.

If something brings us to confess our sin, we discover in that act how good we actually are! Every priest who hears confessions realizes, after a while, that he is not really hearing sins; he is hearing ideals.

The sins are real. But it is impossible for someone to confess a sin as a sin unless something inside that person is better than what the action expresses. We cannot look down on anything unless something in us has risen above it. When David said, "I have sinned against the LORD," he realized that his heart condemned what he had done. In his deepest self, in the person that he truly was, he did not embrace adultery, rape, and murder. Like St. Paul later, he could say, "I see in my members another law at war with the law of my mind, making me captive to the law of sin that dwells in my members." Nevertheless, "In my inmost self I delight in the law of God."[1]

But if he had not said first, "I have sinned against the LORD," he would not have been able to say with the confirming experience of its discovery: "I delight in the law of God."

Every *confession* of sin is a *profession* and discovery of faith. When we pray, *"Create a clean heart in me, O Lord,"* we realize God already has.

In **Mark 4:35-41** Jesus' disciples were aware that he was in the boat with them, but they were not keeping themselves aware of who and what he really was.

First, they assumed Jesus was not aware of what was going on. And in his human nature he may not have been. But he could sleep through a storm because he was always aware he was in the Father's hands. They weren't.

Second, they had ceased to be aware of his love for them. "Teacher, do you not care that we are perishing?" If we are truly aware of God's love and care for us, what can drive away our peace?

When Jesus calmed the sea, they asked one another, "Who then is this?" The answer to that is what we need to recall.

[1] *Romans* 7:22.

Response: How do you habitually think of Jesus? What are you leaving out?

FOR REFLECTION AND DISCUSSION: THIRD WEEK IN ORDINARY TIME

The Power of Light and Love

The reception of God's gift enables us to love as God does.

Invitation: To focus on *awareness* of the love of God that is within us.

For prayer and discussion: How many of these statements do you feel you understand? How often are you consciously aware of them?

Sunday: Christian life on earth is all about growth: growth into clearer light through faith, stronger encouragement through hope, more generous efforts through love. And growth begins with *awareness* of the mystery of God.

Are you *aware* that you were consecrated by God at Baptism to be a *prophet*? To deliver God's message to all you live and work with? Is your community—family, parish, circle of friends—aware of itself as a community of faith, called to reflect on God's words together in order to come to decisions that embody a communal response? What are you doing to make them (and yourself) aware of this?

Monday: True fulfillment is found, always and only, in doing God's will. If we can be satisfied that God wants us to endure what we are enduring, even if God hates it more than we do, we can find peace.

Tuesday: If we let ourselves be *aware* of what God is, we will be impelled to express what we feel. If we do not express it, or express it only in ways that "damn with faint praise," pretty soon we won't feel it anymore.

Wednesday: The core of Paul's preaching: was "the mystery hidden throughout the ages but now revealed to his saints." Through Paul "God chose to make known how great are the riches of this mystery." The mystery, the message Paul was sent to give to the world, is simply this: "*Christ in you*, the hope of glory."

Jesus became alive in Mary as a seed. That same seed is in us by Baptism: the mystery of our lives is the "mystery of Christ in us," growing to "full stature."

Thursday: God created us to "become Christ" by Baptism. To become "in Christ" what Jesus himself is, in a way "far more than all we can ask or imagine."

Friday: We need to have the same "steadfast love" for the Church and for every person on earth that God does.

Saturday: Every *confession* of sin is a *profession* and discovery of faith.

Initiatives:
Write down all you started doing because of others' example. Look twice.
Look always for signs of God's presence before you reject anyone.
Drop your reserves. Express physically what you feel about God.
Cultivate your true self-image. Say the WIT prayer all day long.
Be aware of God's gift. Share it. Sharing will keep you aware.
Don't judge anyone with partial vision. See all with God's eyes.
How do you habitually think of Jesus? What are you leaving out?

SUNDAY FOURTH SUNDAY IN ORDINARY TIME

JANUARY 29, 2012
God Speaks to Us

> *If today you hear his voice, harden not your hearts.*
> (*Responsorial: Psalm* 95)

INVENTORY
Do you ever ask for an interview with God? Do you think he would grant it?

INPUT

In the *Entrance Antiphon* we ask God to "gather us together" from all different cultures ("nations"). This says three things: 1. We see a value in "assembling" with others (The word "church" means "assembly"). 2. We not only accept; we *desire* to mix with people of other nations and cultures. This follows from what we ask for in the *Opening Prayer*: "*to love all people as you love them.*" 3. We gather as unified by something distinctive that we have in common, something different from any particular culture. It is the truth we all see by faith, the way of looking at ourselves, the world, and God that has been revealed to us by Jesus Christ.

What do we gather to do? To "*proclaim your holy name and glory in praising you.*" We in particular need to praise and thank God, because through faith in his revealed word we have received the gift of *knowing God* as he truly is, in a way beyond all human power to know him. Jesus said, "No one knows... the Father except the Son and anyone to whom the Son chooses to reveal him." To know God the Father as one's own Father, you have to *be* God the Son, the "only," the unique Son of the Father. But this has been granted to us because we are "sons and daughters *in the Son.*" We know the Father as Jesus does, because we share in his divine life and his own unique, personal divine act of knowing the Father. Because we are children, God has sent the Spirit of his Son into our hearts, crying, "Abba! Father!" This is our experience of *being* through grace. It is perhaps the deepest experience we have. We need to be *aware* of it.[1]

That is one of the reasons we assemble for Mass. To become aware and keep ourselves aware of who we are, of what we are privileged to know; and of the ensuing possibility of praising God uniquely that makes it our duty to do so. It follows that we need to praise and serve the Father with the perfection of the Son. The *Prayer* leaves no doubt about what that means: "May we serve you with our every desire and *show love for one another* as you have loved us." This is the greatest praise we can give to God.

[1] *Matthew* 11:27; *Galatians* 4:6.

"YOU SPEAK TO US"

In **Deuteronomy 18:15-20** the people tell Moses to go up the mountain and relay to them what God said: "You speak to us, and we will listen; but do not let God speak to us, or we will die."[1]

This sounds strange to us until we realize that we do exactly the same thing! How many of us prefer to let a priest or teacher tell us what the Bible says instead of reading it for ourselves?

We justify this by the fear of "private interpretation" instilled into us for centuries after the Protestant Reformation, when the hierarchy's distrust of an uneducated laity made them discourage Scripture reading. But all that has changed. At Vatican II the bishops were emphatic about it:

> For in the sacred books, the Father who is in heaven meets his children with great love and speaks with them; and the force and power in the word of God is so great that it remains the support and energy of the Church, the strength of faith for her sons and daughters, the food of the soul, the pure and perennial source of spiritual life.

The Church *"earnestly and specifically"* urges *"all the Christian faithful"*

> to learn by frequent reading of the Sacred Scriptures the "excelling knowledge of Jesus Christ." "For ignorance of the Scriptures is ignorance of Christ."[2]

We have the assurance of Scripture that God speaks to each of us:

> O God, from my youth you have taught me,
>
> It is written in the prophets, 'And they shall all be taught by God.'
>
> Now concerning love... you do not need anyone write to you, for you yourselves have been taught by God to love.[3]

The problem is not that God does not speak to us, but that we are unwilling to read his words to hear what he is saying.

A New Teaching

Mark 1:21-28 tells us that Jesus teaches "with authority, not as the scribes."

We know that, like Jesus, the Church teaches "with authority." But what we are not always *aware* of is that the position taken by any individual in the Church, including bishops and the Pope, is not necessarily the teaching of the Church.

The technical word for the official teaching authority in the Church is the *"magisterium."* This includes the bishops and all who teach in their name and as united with them, including theology professors, religion teachers, and preachers in the pulpit. But the Church is careful to distinguish between the extraordinary use of this authority in "infallible" clarifications of doctrine, and the *"ordinary magisterium"* of official teachers who are doing the best they can to apply Church teaching to the problems of the day and to express it in words their particular listeners can understand. They might be addressing second-graders, college professors, or the general public, which differs from country to country and from diocese to diocese. The magisterial teaching of a bishop in a pluralistic or predominately non-Christian diocese might be much more carefully nuanced, for example, than that of a bishop who has only cradle Catholics in mind. Or is fixated on some single issue of local politics.

Even more important are the prejudices and limitations of every human teacher in a particular time and place. Bishops have supported the burning of heretics by the Inquisition, slavery, racial segregation, and some moral standards we find appalling today. It was commonly taught in the period before Vatican II that to miss Mass on one single Sunday was "grave matter" and "mortal sin." You could "go to Hell for a hamburger" if you ate one on

Sunday Fourth Sunday in Ordinary Time

a Friday. This was the unquestioned teaching of the *"ordinary magisterium."*

Recognizing the difference between perennial Church doctrine and current interpretations, the Second Vatican Council urged clergy and laity alike to exercise constant vigilance over what is being taught by words and customs:

> This Synod urges all concerned to work hard to prevent or correct any abuses, excesses or defects which may have crept in here or there, and to restore all things to a more ample praise of Christ and of God.[4]

The first test is conformity to Scripture. It simply is not safe to live only by second-hand knowledge of the word of God. Everyone needs to learn from Jesus himself, who taught "with authority, and not as the scribes."

"I Want You To Be Free"

Most people just won't "take the time" to read or reflect over Scripture. In **1 Corinthians 7:32-35** Paul says, essentially, that this is *idolatry*.

> The married man is anxious about the affairs of the world, how to please his wife, and his *interests are divided*... The married woman is anxious about the affairs of the world, how to please her husband.

Paul might be a little idealistic when he says that, by comparison, "the unmarried... are anxious about the affairs of the Lord, so that they may be holy in body and spirit." Would that were always so! But his point is that to be "divided," whether between pleasing a spouse or a boss, or to be "anxious" about any "affairs of the world," is to have other "gods"—other values, preoccupations and priorities—alongside of God. This is idolatry:

> Hear, O Israel: The LORD is our God, the LORD *alone*. You shall love the LORD your God with *all* your heart, and with *all* your soul, and with *all* your might.

The essence of the lay vocation is to

> seek the kingdom of God by engaging in temporal affairs and by ordering them according to the plan of God. They live in the world; that is, in each and in all of the secular professions and occupations... in the ordinary circumstances of family and social life, from which the very web of their existence is woven.[5]

But the *authenticity* of the lay vocation depends on being able to do this with an undivided heart, focused as single-mindedly on God and the things of God as the most contemplative monk or nun cloistered in a monastery. This means, among other things, that the laity have to *take time* to read and reflect on the word of God. Otherwise they will have nothing to take into the marketplace except what they are marketing.

[1]*Exodus* 20:19.
[2]*On Divine Revelation*, nos. 21, 25, quoting *Philippians* 3-8 and St. Jerome.
[3]*Psalms* 71:17; *John* 6:45; *1 Thessalonians* 4:9.
[4]*The Church*, no. 51.
[5]Vatican II, *The Church*, chapter four.

Insight
Why is every literate Christian obligated to read the word of God?

Initiative
Decide when, where, and how long you will read from Scripture each day.

Fourth Week in Ordinary Time — Monday

January 30, 2012

Lord, rise up and save me!
(*Responsorial: Psalm* 3)

2 Samuel 15:13 to 16:13: When David was fleeing from the revolt of his son Absalom, he was too depressed even to react against Shimei, who was cursing him. When David returned victorious he felt too good to punish him: "Shall anyone be put to death in Israel this day?" But later, when he was dying, he told his son Solomon to "bring Shimei's gray head down with blood to Sheol."[1]

Three different moods; three different choices. This teaches us to *be aware of what we are aware of.*

When David was only aware of betrayal and defeat, he accepted Shimei's insults as part of the package. When he was completely caught up in his triumph, he could forgive them. But when he was aware his end was approaching, he began thinking of unfinished business. Because he did not keep himself *aware* of his moods and allow for them, they made him generous or lethal.

A classic swing in the spiritual life is between "consolation" and "desolation." In consolation we are very aware of the truths of faith, of how good and reliable they are, and of the promises and power that accompany the gift of divine life. We feel joy and peace. In consolation it is easy to serve God. Our awareness puts wind in our sails.

In desolation, all that light is lacking. The truths of faith seem far away and obscure, lacking in credibility and power to motivate. The hard part is that, even if we deliberately remember them and call them into consciousness, they just don't mean anything. Leave us cold. That is when we become aware that we have a free will, and that how we use it is ultimately all that counts in our relationship with God. And with others.

Feelings are not free. Choices are. Feelings have no moral value, good or bad. They may tell us some things about ourselves, but not whether we love God or not. Love is a *choice* that reveals itself in *commitment*. If we are trying to live by love, we do love, regardless of how we feel about it. If we aren't trying to do what love calls for, we are not loving, no matter how much devotion we feel. It is often hard to keep ourselves aware of this, but essential.

God allows "desolation" to make us aware of what comes from us and what from him. We can be very faithful to God when he gives us good feelings. But often when he stops, we stop, which tells us where the power was coming from. When, however, we manage to keep *choosing* to persevere in the good things we were doing, we discover two things: that our feelings are not our real selves; and that even to keep making good free choices we need divine help. This makes us more aware of the gift of God's divine life in us. That is when we say, *"Lord, rise up and save me."*

Mark 5:1-20: The Gerasenes were only aware of the fear they felt and the pigs they lost. It pays to look further.

[1] *2 Samuel* 19:22; *1 Kings* 2:9.

Response: Learn to make yourself aware of gifts you are forgetting about.

Tuesday Fourth Week in Ordinary Time

January 31, 2012

Listen, Lord, and answer me!
(Responsorial: Psalm 86)

2 Samuel 18:9 to 19:3: When Joab, the head of David's army, caught up with David's rebel son, Absalom, who was helplessly entangled in the branches of a tree, he had no scruples about killing him. By killing his prisoner, Joab won the war. But David did not rejoice.

> The king was deeply moved... and wept... "O my son Absalom, my son, my son Absalom! Would I had died instead of you, O Absalom, my son, my son!"
>
> ...So the victory that day was turned into mourning... The troops stole into the city that day as soldiers steal in who are ashamed when they flee in battle.

All Joab thought about was winning the war. David thought about his son. And we are like Joab whenever we kill—whether in war, in executing criminals, or in taking the life of the unborn.

We are so used to "spin" in our society that we take it for granted. We fall into it ourselves. A clear example is the dishonesty of both "pro choice" and "pro life" militants. "Pro-choice" does not include the right to destroy one's own body by suicide or pollute the environment. They are only "pro" the right to kill unborn babies. Dishonest.

Those who call themselves "pro life" are just as dishonest unless they are also "pro" saving the life of condemned criminals by abolishing the death penalty, and of enemies in wars by espousing nonviolence. If not, they have a limited focus. Just like Joab.

Do the parents of those condemned for murder want to see their children executed? How does God feel about it? Or when his children kill his children in war? We are not in tune with God when we celebrate war victories. Even those who believe Christ was excluding war when he said, "Those who want to save their life will lose it," should agree there ought to be no such thing as a victory celebration over the bodies of the dead.[1]

One gets the impression that those who have actually been in combat are the least enthusiastic about celebrating their victory. Their memories are not all joy.

It is a matter of what we choose to be *aware* of. The threat to our well-being posed by a baby in the womb, a criminal in jail, or an enemy at war; or the mystery of the value each has in the eyes of our Father. And the even more overwhelming mystery of God's unlimited, unrestricted love for the innocent and guilty alike. Jesus died for all. His "new commandment" is: "Love one another *as I have loved you*." We need to keep ourselves aware of that.[2]

Mark 5:21-43: Nothing is more tragic than the death of a child. But Jesus was aware that death is simply a pre-resurrection nap—and raised up a twelve-year-old to prove it. To give hope, faith requires *awareness*. And if we keep ourselves aware of the whole mystery of our faith, we may see dying as a better choice than killing.

[1] This is one of the texts repeated word-for-word in *Matthew* (16:25), *Mark* (8:35) and *Luke* (9:24).
[2] *John* 13:34; 15:12. And see the story of the "prodigal son," *Luke* 15:11-32.

Response: Open your eyes to the Christian understanding of life and death.

Fourth Week in Ordinary Time — Wednesday

February 1, 2012

Lord, forgive the wrong I have done!
(Responsorial: Psalm 32)

2 Samuel 24:2-17 bewilders us. Why would God punish David so severely—and send such suffering on his people—just because he took a census?

Our bewilderment reveals a deep and serious flaw in the way we were taught morality. David's sin was that he was gratifying his love of *power*. Like a miser counting money, he wanted to gloat over how many troops he could put in the field. Even Joab tried to warn him: "Why does my lord the king want to do this?" But we were never warned against this sin or its dangers.

We were made very aware of the obvious sins: lying, stealing, uncommitted sex, etc. But no one alerted us to the greater sin, more dangerous and damaging than all the above: love of *power*. Those attached to power bring down destruction on themselves and on all who are affected by their exercise of authority. Lord Acton said, "Power corrupts, and absolute power corrupts absolutely."[1] It corrupts, not only those who enjoy it, but the whole community—family, institution, civil society, or Church—that depends on their decisions for good government. Power by nature tends to blind the mind and deaden the heart. No one is exempt: government officials, ecclesiastical authorities, corporate executives or spouses (male or female) addicted to dominance: all are in danger. All who have power "thrust upon them" should walk in fear and trembling. Power corrupts. Those who do not fear it are probably already corrupted.

They didn't teach us this in grade school. We are reaping the results.

God's treatment of David was to warn us that, when authorities are in love with their power, both they and their communities suffer. In **Mark 6:1-6** we see that Jesus taught this by giving the opposite example. When he

> came to his hometown… many who heard him were astounded. They said, "Where did this man get all this?… What deeds of power are being done by his hands! Is not this the carpenter, the son of Mary…?"

Jesus made no display of power growing up. He shunned it. The power he finally began to use in his ministry was the power to heal. And that was normally a response to faith:

> He could do no deed of power there, except that he laid his hands on a few sick people and cured them.

He was emphatic with his disciples:

> You know that the rulers of the Gentiles lord it over them…. It will not be so among you; but whoever wishes to be great among you must be your servant…

St. Peter echoed Jesus, writing as a fellow "elder" to priests and bishops:

> Do not lord it over those in your charge, but be examples to the flock…. Clothe yourselves with humility in your dealings with one another, for "God opposes the proud, but gives grace to the humble."[2]

We must remain *aware* of this. Or else.

---

[1] He wrote this in a letter to Bishop Mandell Creighton, 1887, after Vatican I had declared that the Pope had absolute power in the Church.
[2] *Matthew* 20:25-27; *1 Peter* 5:1-5.

Response: Measure your power over others. Ask how it makes you feel. React.

THURSDAY FEAST OF THE PRESENTATION OF THE LORD

FEBRUARY 2, 2012

Also called: The Purification of Mary and "Candlemas"

"The light of revelation to the nations, the glory of your people."

> *Who is this King of Glory? It is the Lord!*
> *(Psalm 24)*

INVENTORY

How has Christ been presented to you? Does he present himself now in the same way he did originally? How do you present yourself to him?

INPUT

The *Entrance Antiphon* (*Psalm* 48:10-11) assumes that God presents himself to us in church, and especially that Jesus does. But we can miss this if we do not deliberately make ourselves *aware* of it. We need to remind ourselves of what is going on and *think*. "Within your temple *we ponder* your loving kindness, O God."

In the three Mass prayers Jesus is presented to us in three different ways. In the *Opening Prayer* he *purifies*: we ask the Father to let him "free our hearts from sin and bring us into your presence." In the *Prayer Over the Gifts* he *gives us divine life*: the mystery of Baptism and the Mass is that Jesus "offered himself as a Lamb without blemish for the life of the world" and united us to himself in that offering. In the *Prayer after Communion* we recognize that Communion is a preview of the "wedding banquet of the Lamb" that *strengthens our hope* and "prepares us to meet Christ when he comes."

"A REFINER'S FIRE...."

Malachi 3:1-4 reminds us that we may not be ready to accept Jesus as he really is. His own People weren't, in spite of the centuries of preparation God had given them. Even his chosen disciples were not able to accept his way of saving the world when he told them about it.[1] And people today—perhaps the majority of Christians—still resist any teaching that calls them beyond the morality of "good human behavior." Where real faith in God's word is required to go against or beyond cultural attitudes, values, and practices, Christians tend to conform, like everyone else, to the going standards of their peer group.

The real problem is not the sins Christians commit, but the fact they are closed to going beyond just "being good." They are not listening to the call to be *divine*. For example, some are very vocal against abortion. This is good, but does not require any faith. Any decent human being whose mind has not been distorted by the pseudo-intellectualism of our culture knows abortion is wrong. Christians who fight against abortion are showing their human decency, not their faith. What would they be vocal about if they had really absorbed the Beatitudes and the Sermon on the Mount? Where do we hear Christian voices raised in favor of that love of neighbor Jesus taught? (The answer, it seems, is in the less-read, more serious publications that are not considered "safe" enough to be offered in parish vestibules.)

Those who apply radical Gospel principles to public life are accused first of preaching "politics" and then of being "liberals." So we cannot use as examples Church teaching about the death penalty, "pre-emptive strike" wars (such as Iraq), unjustifiable affluence, international marketing responsibility, health care, immigration reform, and "social justice" issues in general. People will ignore, rather than accuse, the popes and bishops who speak out about these issues, but they will turn on anyone who quotes them.

So let's look at where it begins: in the individual heart. The "purification" Malachi calls for (with John of the Cross) is purification from the inertia of clinging to gradeschool morality. We have to confront the Gospel as adults and let it confront us. For starters, try:

> We are obliged to support the poor and not just from our surplus.
>
> Moderation and simplicity ought to become the criteria of our daily lives.
>
> Money ought not to be used for war, nor for destroying and killing, but for defending the dignity of human beings, for improving their life and for building a truly open, free and harmonious society.
>
> Christ's *example*, no less than his words, is *normative* for Christians.
>
> The Gospel invites believers not to accumulate the goods of this passing world... This is a *duty intrinsic to the Christian vocation*, no less than the *duty of working to overcome poverty*. Those who are poor in the Gospel sense are ready to sacrifice their resources and their own selves so that others may live.
>
> Both the commandments and Jesus' invitation to the rich young man stand at the service of *a single and indivisible charity, which spontaneously tends towards that perfection whose measure is God alone*: "You, therefore, must be perfect, as your heavenly Father is perfect."
>
> Jesus' *way of acting* and his words, his deeds and his precepts constitute the *moral rule of Christian life*. Indeed, his actions, and in particular his Passion and Death on the Cross [reveal] exactly the love that Jesus wishes to be imitated by all who follow him. It is "the 'new' commandment."[2]

How often do we find this teaching developed in popular preaching and publications? How inclined do you yourself feel now to reflect on it deeply?

WHAT ARE YOU WAITING FOR?

Different people react in different ways to encounter with Christ. And we all react differently at different times in our lives. In **Luke 2:22-40** Simeon's first reaction was joy that he was finally seeing what he had been waiting for. This says something about his habitual *awareness*.

Simeon's underlying consciousness in life was characterized by expectation. Whatever he had, enjoyed or was suffering, that was not his main focus. His heart was focused on a fulfillment he believed in, hoped for, and desired

Thursday Feast of the Presentation of the Lord

with the first love of his heart. He wanted more than he could find on this earth; or, more precisely, he wanted to find on this earth, here and now, something this world alone cannot make available. He wanted to see that fulfillment, that "salvation," that could only be God's "saving deed." Without knowing it, what he really wanted was to see God made flesh. And he saw him.

This invites us to ask what our most constant, underlying hope is. What are we subconsciously—or consciously—waiting for? How has this changed through the years? What is it now?

Children wait for the recess bell to ring, for lunch or dinner, for toys at Christmas. Adolescents may take a longer view. They wait for someone to ask them for a date, for graduation, for recognition from others. Young adults look forward to getting a job or a promotion; to buying a house, paying off their loans. As we get older we may look forward to grandchildren, to retirement, or even to release from this world in death. The question is, how strong is our desire, our hope, to encounter Christ? Or, in the words of the song, to "see him more clearly, follow him more nearly, love him more dearly"? How strong, how conscious, is our sense of *expectation*? And is it the fulfillment promised by God that we look forward to?

Simeon proclaimed Jesus "a revealing light to the nations and the glory of your people Israel." But he also warned that Jesus would lead people into crisis. Not all would welcome the challenge of his light: "This child is destined to be the downfall and the rise of many in Israel, a sign that will be opposed."

Everyone who encounters Jesus will have to take a stance toward him. He came, not only to reveal himself, but to reveal each one of us to ourselves: "so that the thoughts of many hearts may be laid bare." Jesus said that he himself "judges no one." Rather he *is* the judgment. The response we make to him is the judgment pronounced on what we are, what our hearts desire, what we choose to be and become.[3]

God is not indifferent to our choice. What Simeon foretold of Mary, that the rejection of her son would be like a sword piercing her own heart, is infinitely more true of the grief our Father feels when those he calls to be his sons and daughters reject his Son. And reject the life they can have in him.

One Like Us

We may fear an encounter with Christ that challenges us to live on the level of God. So **Hebrews 2:14-18** reassures us that the one who invites us, Jesus,

> had to become like his brothers and sisters in every way, so that he might be a merciful and faithful high priest.... Since he was himself tested through what he suffered, he is able to help those who are tempted.

Jesus brought divine living down to ground level by living in every way as a human. We just need to *consciously* let him act *with* us, *in* us and *through* us.

[1]*Matthew* 16:21-23.
[2]Pope John Paul II, "World Day of Peace" address, January 1, 1993; *The Splendor of Truth*, nos. 18-21.
[3]*John* 8:15; 9:39; 12:31-50.

Response: Welcome the real Jesus. Say the WIT prayer all day long.

The Commemoration of St. Blaise, Bishop and Martyr — Friday

February 3, 2012

Blessed be God, my salvation!
(*Responsorial: Psalm 18*)

Sirach 47:2-11: What is striking about Sirach's praise of David is that after each accomplishment he lists, he tells us what David was *aware* of. When he slew Goliath, he "called on the Lord Most High." He was aware of who "gave strength to his right arm." In all the battles he won, "he gave thanks to the Holy One." He "put all his heart into his songs, out of love for his Maker." He enhanced the singing and music at feasts "causing the Lord's holy name to be praised." And so "the Lord took away his sins" and "exalted him forever."

God looks to the heart. And so should we. We "put our heart into" what we are doing when we act with conscious faith, remembering who we are as children of the Father, sharing in his divine life through identification with the Son. Conscious of his prolonged creative word, "Beeee…" sustaining us in existence. Of the gift of his Spirit within us, empowering us to act on the level of God through faith, hope, and love. Aware that we are enlightened, called, and sent by God to continue the mission of Jesus. Aware of Jesus himself within us, expressing his truth, his love, in and through our human words and actions, to give and enhance his divine life in all we deal with. Aware that Jesus has won the victory, has conquered sin and death, and is establishing his reign now through our efforts as "stewards of his kingship." To keep ourselves *aware* of the mystery of our ongoing, interactive relationship with God is the first phase of our journey into the "fullness of life" and the "perfection of love."[1]

The refrain of our hearts should be always: "*Blessed be God, my salvation!* Lord, do this *with* me, do this *in* me, do this *through* me."

In **Mark 6:14-29** even Herod, spiritually numbed though he was by immersion in sensuality, power, and prestige, was able to feel a prophetic suspicion approaching truth when he heard what Jesus was doing. "John [the Baptizer]," he said, "whom I beheaded, has been raised."

He was right about the resurrection; just wrong in his timing and identification of the one who had been raised. What Herod saw in Jesus was divine life at work. And he would see it again in the disciples of Jesus after Jesus, not John, whom Herod, with Pilate, sent to the cross, was raised from the dead. The life and actions of those who have died and been raised with Christ through Baptism are inexplicable without the recognition of grace. It is only by sharing in the divine life of Jesus, risen and living in them, that Christians can live as the Gospel calls us to live. What Herod saw in Jesus, everyone on earth should see in his followers.

If they don't, the first reason is that Christians themselves are just not *aware* of the mystery of their being. That is the first thing we need to work on.

[1] See *John* 10:10; 16:33; *Romans*, chapters 5 to 8. Vatican II, *The Church*, no. 40.

Response: Keep reminding yourself of whom and what you have become by grace.

SATURDAY FOURTH WEEK IN ORDINARY TIIME

FEBRUARY 4, 2012

Lord, teach me your decrees.
(Responsorial: Psalm 119)

The introductory verses to **1 Kings 3:4-13** tell us that "the people were sacrificing at the high places," the hilltop shrines where the pagans sacrificed to idols. They did it, however, "because no house had yet been built for the name of the LORD." And Solomon himself, though he "loved the LORD, walking in the statutes of his father David" also "sacrificed and offered incense at the high places." This was good and bad.

We can compare this to Catholics who have abandoned the Mass to worship in Protestant services. This is good, because they are worshiping sincerely with true Christian believers in authentically Christian assemblies (the word "church" means "assembly"). But it is also bad, because they are not in the "House built for the name of the Lord" where Eucharist is celebrated and the "catholic, universal faith that comes to us from the apostles" is preached in union with all the bishops throughout the world. Why aren't they?

Catholics go to Protestant churches for the same reason the Jews sacrificed in the "high places" when "no house had yet been built for the name of the Lord." They go because we do not provide them with a parish where they can find what Jesus offers and they seek.

The essentials are present, of course, in every Catholic parish: instruction, preaching, all seven sacraments, the Mass, and even, for those who know how to recognize it, a community of faith. It would be heresy to deny this. But to say realistically, in practical terms, that all Catholics can find what they need in their parishes would be to bury our heads in the ground. The second largest religious "denomination" in the United States, after the Catholics, are the ex-Catholics. When the most popular Protestant churches report that 40% of their congregations grew up as Catholics, we would be blinding ourselves to say we have really "built a house for the Lord" where they can find him. Whose fault is this?

Ultimately, of course, it is the Pope's. Since over the centuries the popes have reserved to themselves many pastoral decisions that properly belong to the local bishops—for example, the regulation of liturgy and the requirements for ordination—the Pope has to say, like every "monovocal" authority, "The buck stops here."

Then, in descending order, we blame the bishops and pastors. But this is a cop-out. All the popes, bishops, and pastors together cannot provide an adequate experience of God at Sunday Mass unless the congregation—the *congregation*, the congregation—are expressing their faith enthusiastically, joyfully, and credibly. God has called every baptized Catholic, as he called Solomon, to "build me a house."

The first step is to be *aware*, when we walk in for Mass, that the effect the liturgy will have on many depends, in large part, on how we participate in it.

In **Mark 6:30-34** the disciples return from their mission tour and tell Jesus "all that they had done and taught." In response he takes them away "to a deserted place by themselves" to

Fourth Week in Ordinary Time Saturday

build up their union with himself. But when he saw the crowd that sought them out, he realized that all the ordained priests and bishops in the world would never be enough. "He saw a great crowd; and he had compassion for them, because they were like sheep without a shepherd."

The word "pastor" means "shepherd." But no pastor can possibly be an adequate shepherd for a whole parish. He would need more "gifts of the Holy Spirit" than the catechisms can describe. When Paul said, "I have become all things to all people," he did not mean he could be and do everything that each person required. That is why he made it clear that to each and every one "the manifestation of the Spirit is given for the common good," to "equip the saints for the work of ministry, for building up the body of Christ."[1]

Paul gives only a "short list" of all the gifts, services, and activities needed to bring about the "common good" in a Christian community. No one person, and specifically, no ordained priest or bishop, could possibly have them all. It takes the work of every member to "build a house for the Lord" where all of his people can find him. That is why Paul goes on to use the phrase "building up" or "to build up" five more times in the same letter. It is a basic Christian obligation, rooted in our baptismal anointing as "priests," to "build a house for the Lord" by building up the Church, beginning in our own parish. Not to do this (okay, here comes the bombshell!) is just as truly a violation of our baptismal promises as failing to communicate deeply with a spouse is a violation of the marriage vows. When are we going to start taking our commitments seriously? All of them.

The last statement may sound harsh. It isn't. It is challenging. So is an invitation to compete in the Olympics. All of us are "volunteer Christians," and we are all Christians by invitation only. Jesus Christ has chosen us to be his body, to let him live, speak, and act in us to continue his mission on earth. We did not choose him; he chose us, and has anointed us to "bear fruit, fruit that will last forever." But having been chosen, and having been promised a "posterity" in those who have received or grown in divine life through our ministries, it is obvious that we need to live up to what we are, have become, and are called to be. And to do.[2]

Is it harsh, is it a threat to tell fathers and mothers they are "committed" to take care of their children? Or do parents consider this the greatest privilege and blessing of their lives? It is the same for us who are called to take care of the children of God as co-sharers in the life of the Father. We just need to keep ourselves *aware* of the mystery of our being, the mystery of our life, the mystery of our identification with Jesus, "only Son of the Father," the mystery of what it means to be and live as a Christian.

[1] *1 Corinthians* 9:22; 12:1-10; 14:4-26; *Ephesians* 4:11-13.
[2] *John* 15:16.

Response: Decide to cultivate *awareness* of who you are and are called to be. Don't just dismiss this; make a concrete decision. *How will you do this?*

FOR REFLECTION AND DISCUSSION: FOURTH WEEK IN ORDINARY TIME

God Speaks to Us.

The word God speaks always brings forth life.

Invitation: To make a difference through response, like those Scripture praises.

For prayer and discussion: How many of these statements do you feel you understand? How often are you consciously aware of them?

Sunday: Our experience of *being* through grace is the deepest experience we have. We know the Father as Jesus does, because we share in his divine life and his own unique act of knowing the Father. "Because we are children, God has sent the Spirit of his Son into our hearts, crying, "Abba! Father!" We need to be *aware* of this.

Recognizing the difference between perennial Church doctrine and current interpretations, the Second Vatican Council urged clergy and laity alike to exercise constant vigilance over what is being taught by words and customs.

Monday: Love is a *choice* that reveals itself in *commitment*. If we are trying to live by love, we do love, regardless of how we feel about it.

Tuesday: Jesus' "new commandment" is: "Love one another *as I have loved you*." He died for all. We need to keep ourselves aware of that.

Wednesday: Power by nature tends to blind the mind and deaden the heart. No one is exempt: government officials, ecclesiastical authorities, corporate executives or spouses (male or female) addicted to dominance—all are in danger.

Thursday: Simeon's underlying consciousness in life was characterized by expectation. Whatever he had, enjoyed, or was suffering, that was not his main focus. His heart was focused on a fulfillment he believed in, hoped for, and desired with the first love of his heart.

Friday: God looks to the heart. And so should we.

To keep ourselves *aware* of the mystery of our ongoing, interactive relationship with God—*Our Father...in heaven*— is the first phase of our journey into the "fullness of life" and the "perfection of love."

Saturday: The first step is to be *aware*, when we walk in for Mass, that the effect the liturgy will have on others depends, in large part, on how we participate in it.

Initiatives:
Decide when, where, and how long you will read from Scripture each day.
Learn to make yourself aware of gifts you are forgetting about.
Open your eyes to the Christian understanding of life and death.
Measure your power over others. Ask how it makes you feel. React.
Welcome the real Jesus. Say the WIT prayer all day long.
Embody some characteristics in your lifestyle that reveal it as divine.
Keep reminding yourself of who and what you have become by grace.
Decide to cultivate *awareness* of who you are and are called to be.

WHAT HAS THIS BOOKLET DONE FOR YOU?

When we are on a journey it encourages us to look back and see how much ground we have covered, how far we have advanced. So let's do that. Remember, the effectiveness of input is measured by the authenticity of output.

What did these reflections do for you? What did you do in response to them?

The reflections during Advent and the Christmas Season were designed to help you deepen your appreciation of the first phrase of the *Our Father*—"*Our Father…in heaven,*" which presents the first mystery of Baptism: the *new identity* we have "in Christ" as "sons and daughters of the Father." Did they do that?

The reflections also developed the first phase of our journey into living the Christian life fully. The first phase is to cultivate *awareness* of the mystery of the divine life that Baptism gave us. Have you become more aware of that mystery throughout your day?

More specifically:

- Did you read the reflections:
    - daily?   • at least once a week?   • three or more times a week?

- Did they help you understand better the mystery of divine life? Of being a real son or daughter of the Father? Of being this because you have "become Christ" by Baptism?

- During this season have you become more *conscious* of the mystery of calling God your Father? More *aware* of being divine?

- Did these reflections lead you to make any *decisions*; for example, to begin your day with the WIT prayer and say it all day long? To pray the *Our Father* daily?

- Have you profited from them enough to recommend these reflections to others?